The European Union's Trade Policies and their Economic Effects

OECD

ORGANISATION FOR ECONOMIC CO-OPERATION AND DEVELOPMENT

ORGANISATION FOR ECONOMIC CO-OPERATION AND DEVELOPMENT

Pursuant to Article 1 of the Convention signed in Paris on 14th December 1960, and which came into force on 30th September 1961, the Organisation for Economic Co-operation and Development (OECD) shall promote policies designed:

- to achieve the highest sustainable economic growth and employment and a rising standard of living in Member countries, while maintaining financial stability, and thus to contribute to the development of the world economy;
- to contribute to sound economic expansion in Member as well as non-member countries in the process of economic development; and
- to contribute to the expansion of world trade on a multilateral, non-discriminatory basis in accordance with international obligations.

The original Member countries of the OECD are Austria, Belgium, Canada, Denmark, France, Germany, Greece, Iceland, Ireland, Italy, Luxembourg, the Netherlands, Norway, Portugal, Spain, Sweden, Switzerland, Turkey, the United Kingdom and the United States. The following countries became Members subsequently through accession at the dates indicated hereafter: Japan (28th April 1964), Finland (28th January 1969), Australia (7th June 1971), New Zealand (29th May 1973), Mexico (18th May 1994), the Czech Republic (21st December 1995), Hungary (7th May 1996), Poland (22nd November 1996) and Korea (12th December 1996). The Commission of the European Communities takes part in the work of the OECD (Article 13 of the OECD Convention).

Publié également en français.

Preface

This book is an updated and revised version of a paper that was presented as background documentation for a seminar held at the OECD headquarters on 12 December 1997. The authors are Peter Hoeller, Nathalie Girouard and Alessandra Colecchia. We would like to thank Stephen Potter, Val Koromzay, Jorgen Elmeskov, Anthony Kleitz, Günter Keil, Barbara Fliess, Steve Thomsen, Marie-France Houde, Pierre Poret, Eirikur Einarsson and Dimitris Diakosavvas for many helpful comments and suggestions. We would also like to thank the colleagues at the European Commission for their co-operation. We are grateful for the contribution of George Soumelis and Emma Chas in the early stage of this project. Finally, we are indebted to Desney Erb for statistical assistance and to Celia Rutkoski and Hervé Bource for secretarial skills.

The views expressed in this book are those of the authors and do not necessarily reflect those of the governments of the OECD or the European Commission. This book is published on the responsibility of the Secretary-General of the OECD.

Table of contents

Tables

Annexes

Figures

Summary

Already the Treaty of Rome called for internal and external liberalisation

Forty years ago, external protection was high in most countries and Europe was comprised of many "trade fortresses". The founders of the Community shared a coherent economic policy view, with the Treaty of Rome calling for an internal market with no obstacles to trade and strong competition, as well as for multilateral liberalisation. This publication retraces the external liberalisation efforts, discusses the current trade regime in international comparison, and sets out the Community's future trade agenda. A key aim of the study will be to clarify and, where feasible, to quantify the economic effects of the European Union's (EU) trade policies.

Decision-making on foreign trade policy is largely centralised at the EU level

Partly by necessity, partly by design, the EU's trade policy has been "walking on two legs" since its early days: multilateral liberalisation and regional integration. The long-standing pursuit of deeper integration and enlargement, and the involvement in regional preferential agreements makes the EU's experience unique. Another unique feature is the institutional set-up. While largely prepared by the Commission, major decisions are taken by the Council (for trade in goods and part of services). Some competencies are shared between the Union and the Member States. However, the negotiation and decision making process is not different between the areas of mixed or exclusive competence. Centralisation of most decisions on foreign trade policy at the EU level is necessary to ensure the functioning of the internal market. Centralisation should, in principle, strengthen the EU's position in international trade matters. Whether a strong negotiating position is a good thing for its trading partners depends on the position the negotiating "club" is taking, for instance, whether it pursues an inward or outward looking agenda. In addition to the size of the club, its "quality" matters: if club members push different views, slow decision making or paralysis could be the consequence.

Internal integration has probably not hampered multilateral liberalisation

Since its creation, the European Union has actively participated in multilateral liberalisation efforts. Whether the creation and expansion of the European Union has speeded up or slowed down such efforts is impossible to tell. Many commentators argue that the creation of the European Economic Community (EEC) led directly to the Dillon and Kennedy Rounds, as other countries were concerned by the trade diversion consequences. On the other hand, the Community successfully resisted for decades the inclusion of agriculture in trade liberalisation negotiations. Also other countries have at times resisted liberalisation efforts and deep integration in Europe shows that a vast regional integration scheme does not necessarily undermine the multilateral trading system.

The coincidence of multilateral and bilateral liberalisation makes the assessment of economic effects difficult

While it is clear that trade barriers have come down considerably across a wide range of sectors, it is very difficult to compare trade regimes across countries and assess their economic effects. This is so, because the distance of a country's trade regime from an "ideal" world of free trade cannot be measured in the absence of comprehensive empirical measures of effective protection. In addition, while a feature of multilateralism is the absence of discrimination among trading partners, another one is how close a country's trade regime comes to approximate free trade. If a country opened markets to just one small country that would seem to decrease multilateralism, but opening trade to all countries but a small one would seem to increase it. Given the large number of bilateral trade agreements, the latter aspect is of considerable importance for the European Union.

Tariffs have come down, but EU consumers could still benefit a lot from further liberalisation of trade in agricultural and textile products

Taking the modest route of comparing trade policy indicators nevertheless provides plenty of insights. In particular, most-favoured-nation tariffs on most goods have fallen considerably, to levels which probably are more a nuisance than a barrier to trade. However, tariffs on textiles and apparel still remain rather high – a feature also found elsewhere in the OECD – and the high level of agricultural protection has not declined, despite efforts to reform the Common Agricultural Policy (CAP). Contrary to developments in the Union, agricultural protection has shown a trend decline in many other OECD countries, even though in most countries protection has drifted up again in recent years, in line with developments in the Union. The tariffication process of agricultural and food products agreed upon in the Uruguay Round raised measures of average tariff rates, and high rates of tariffs across a wide range of products probably imply that agricultural imports will be only little affected even after the phasing in of the Uruguay Agreement on Agriculture. However, market access has improved to some extent due to minimum access requirements and a sizeable reduction in export subsidies has been phased in. While the Agenda 2000 reform in anticipation of the widening of the Union will deepen and extend the 1992 CAP reform, it is uncertain whether it will be sufficient to resolve the problem of exportable surpluses for some commodities. Consumers in the Union could benefit considerably from a further substantial liberalisation of trade in agricultural and textile products.

The Union is a frequent user of non-tariff barriers and of the WTO dispute settlement mechanism

Non-tariff border measures have traditionally been more prevalent in the Union and the United States than in Japan or Canada. The textile sector remains the most protected by non-tariff barriers, while tariffication implied a sharp fall in the pervasiveness of such barriers for agricultural products and in the processed food sector. Concerning anti-dumping and other price control measures, the Union is a major user, second only to the United States. In contrast, Japan has hardly used such measures at all. The European Union changed anti-dumping legislation in 1994, while revising other provisions such as those on circumvention. The new regulation provides for fairer price comparisons, stricter injury requirements and for a broader role of the "Community interest test" but, even after these changes, proving the existence of unfair trade practices has remained highly contentious. The European Union, with the United States, is a frequent user of the World Trade Organisation (WTO) dispute settlement mechanism. While many disputes could be settled without creating frictions, some have led to serious tensions, most prominent being the banana case, EU imports of hormone-treated beef and of genetically-modified food.

The liberalisation of services is still in its infancy, but gains could be substantial

Multilateral liberalisation of services is still in its infancy, but got a strong boost from the General Agreement on Trade in Services. Assessing the openness of service sectors across countries is very murky and only very crude indicators are available. Despite the long history of sheltering certain service sectors, such as airlines, telecommunications and certain professions, internal liberalisation due to the single market initiative has also improved external access. Liberalisation efforts in Europe continue, to varying degrees across sectors, and could lay the ground for a liberal EU position in the next multilateral services round. Gains from multilateral liberalisation of services trade could dwarf that of further liberalisation of goods industries. The European Union has also launched an e-commerce strategy to catch up with the United States in this area.

Trade liberalisation has boosted growth...

Growth and labour market effects of trade liberalisation are close to the heart of current policy debates. While it was accepted wisdom earlier on that a strong correlation exists between trade and growth, more recent research suggests that the apparent direct link could be spurious. However, trade could still affect growth indirectly through positive effects on capital formation in a broad sense. This study indeed finds a sizeable growth effect for a trade openness indicator and a smaller additional effect coming from rising intra-industry trade, probably reflecting trade-induced scale economies and better specialisation due to the greater variety of available inputs. Moreover, it also found that it is openness in general, rather than regional trade integration that has favoured growth in Europe.

... but labour market rigidities may have forestalled even larger gains

A fast-growing body of research has focused on the wage and employment effects of rising competition from low wage countries. While some studies found little effect, in line with research concerning the United States, others tell a more cautionary tale: the effect would largely depend on labour market institutions. Indeed, slow restructuring in some European countries could lower the benefits induced by trade liberalisation, with gains from freer trade being largely used to compensate those who have lost their job. On the other hand, the labour market effects may not be unfavourable over the medium term, as a lowering in rents could lead to weaker insider power and make labour markets more flexible. Given the different labour market institutions within Europe, the trade and employment story is probably country-specific.

External and internal liberalisation have gone hand in hand

Internal integration in the European Union has progressed in waves and the integrated trading area has expanded from the original six to the current fifteen countries. The single market programme was the latest initiative to remove the remaining obstacles to trade. Overall, access of third countries has improved over a wide range of sectors and products. National quotas have been removed and only a few have been replaced at the Union level, barriers to establishment have been lowered and most services are undergoing major liberalisation. Overall, the parallel, interactive nature of external liberalisation and internal integration has to be emphasised. However, there are still areas, which continue to be strongly sheltered at the national level, largely because policy changes occurred only recently. This is the case, for example, for public procurement and professional services. In other areas, policy changes at the EU level have been timid or non-existent so far. Examples are liberalisation efforts concerning postal services or railways, even though some Member countries have made considerable progress in raising competitive pressures in these sectors. Also the internal market is not entirely in place, with company law being an important area still to be dealt with. Overall, both potential external and internal competitors suffer to the same extent from these shortcomings. There is, however, one exception: the public procurement directives contain a small Union preference.

The number of regional trade agreements has proliferated

Following a period of relative quiescence, the number of regional trade agreements has risen considerably in the past decade (27 countries were covered in 1970, but close to 100 currently), with another 40 countries receiving unilateral concessions under the Generalised System of Preferences (GSP). They provide for different levels of trade liberalisation, from deep integration in Europe over bilateral preferential agreements down to non-reciprocal agreements with many African, Caribbean and Pacific countries. Apart from reaping the gains from freer trade, political concerns have also provided a strong impetus to the proliferation of trade agreements. Indeed, especially in Europe and the surrounding area, trade agreements are part of a broader political agenda, which aims at creating a large, prosperous, stable and democratic area. Co-operation is not limited to trade, but also includes a considerable amount of funds flowing from the European Union to its partner countries.

Trade diversion due to regional trade agreements has probably become minor

Countries outside the EU's regional agreements have often voiced concerns about the possibility that trade diversion could outweigh trade creation – an inherent possible problem in any free-trade area arrangement. While the General Agreement on Tariffs and Trade (GATT) provides guidance – agreements must free "substantially all trade" and external trade barriers ought not be raised – it has always been difficult to reach agreement on the conformity with GATT requirements, or on the compensation for changes in bound tariffs. On the other hand, none of the agreements has been disapproved explicitly. Assessing the economic effects empirically is also a difficult issue, as the counterfactual state of the world without regional agreements is not known. An assessment based on manufacturing sector import penetration ratios suggests that, since 1970, internal import penetration rose about as fast as external import penetration, while the share of domestic production in apparent consumption fell. Double trade creation (internal and external) does not, however, permeate all sectors and regions. Notable exceptions are the food, drink and tobacco industries and non-ferrous metals, while external import penetration rose considerably in the textile, footwear and leather sectors, despite heavy protection. Overall, any bias against extra-EU imports was probably minor. Also, other trade indicators do not suggest that the Union is an outlier (its share of trade in GDP is somewhat higher than that of the United States or Japan, for instance) and it is also difficult to find evidence of diversion of foreign direct investment. This is to be expected, because external protection in the manufacturing industries was already low in the early seventies and the internal market for goods fairly well integrated. Academic work suggests that some trade diversion may have occurred between the creation of the EEC and the late 1960s, a time when the difference between external and internal protection was still considerably higher.

Recent regional trade agreements take other countries' concerns better into account

Except for the well-documented case of the agricultural area, trade diversion should currently be of little concern for the Union's trading partners because a low level of overall protection has been achieved. But there is some risk of trade diversion as a result of the agreements between the European Union and the eastern European and Mediterranean countries. Some of them still have very high levels of protection and rules of origin have intensified potential diversion risks. However, for those countries, which will join the Union, tariffs are set to decline considerably. It should also be recognised in this context that the European Union has made a considerable effort over the years to better reflect concerns of third parties: recent agreements provide for reciprocal industrial free trade over shorter transition periods; agriculture is included, even though the ambition to liberalise remains weak; many agreements also cover services; and the European Union encourages countries both to join the World Trade Organisation and to liberalise trade unilaterally. Finally, rules of origin have changed recently to a European-wide cumulation system, which implies that imported inputs can now be sourced in 28 European countries to produce an originating product.

The future agenda is multilateral and regional, and also focuses on trade-related issues

Given the impetus to form free trade agreements also in America and Asia, the issue of trade creation versus trade diversion is relevant not just with regard to the EU initiatives. More broadly, there is concern that the trading world will fragment into a tripolar constellation. Recent research shows that this could theoretically be a global welfare-minimising solution and that the impetus for the trading blocs to pursue multilateral liberalisation could vanish. While the theoretical arguments are well taken, the medium-term trade agenda of the Union shows that there is currently little risk that it will start looking inwards or pursue aggressive unilateralism. Indeed, the EU's trade policy is now "walking on three legs": it intends to pursue multilateral liberalisation actively; to deepen integration with the eastern European and Mediterranean countries; and to strengthen co-operation on trade-related issues with major trading partners.

Co-operation on trade-related issues with other countries has been stepped up

While the World Trade Organisation received a mandate to work on new trade issues, the European Union is pressing ahead with bilateral agreements, as multilateral progress will probably be slow. The European Union is very well placed to show the way forward, because it itself has had to grapple with cross-border policy spillover issues over the last 40 years in implementing the internal market. In the competition policy field, countries who want to join the Union will have to implement competition laws modelled on EU rules. With other countries, such as the United States, co-operation has advanced, and is largely based on the exchange of information. While many cases have been handled on a mutually satisfactory basis, recent experience shows that not all trade frictions can be avoided. The current agreement with the United States is a timid start as compared with the Commission's broader long-term views on global competition policies as it promotes a multilateral agreement on minimum competition standards, enforcement mechanisms and mutual assistance. The European Union has, for instance, recommended the creation of a framework in which the members of the World Trade Organisation would enforce their own competition rules based on commonly adopted principles. In a similar vein, the European Union is pursuing the elimination of technical barriers to trade, an area in which it has gained considerable experience through the single market. The Union has struck several agreements on conformity assessment, covering key industrial sectors. These agreements allow trading costs to be reduced, but may raise access problems for those outside the agreement. A key issue in this context is confidence in each partner's certification procedures.

The future enlargement implies a considerable reform effort by applicant countries and by the Union itself

The central and eastern European countries (CEECs) regard membership of the European Union as vital and accession negotiations have begun with ten CEECs. Negotiations have also started with Cyprus and Malta, and Turkey has been added to the list of accession candidates. Important groundwork has been laid with the Europe Agreements, with Interim Agreements phasing in bilateral free trade areas for non-agricultural products over a ten-year period and providing also for some liberalisation of agricultural trade. The Agreements contain many additional provisions, which aim at the approximation of economic rules in these countries to those of the European Union. Current levels of protection for industrial goods in some CEECs are considerably above EU levels, while agricultural protection is much lower. Accession of these countries poses a major challenge to the European Union: there are large differences between applicant countries and the European Union; these countries would all be net recipients of EU funds; and the Amsterdam Summit made no progress in reforming the EU's institutions. Commission scenarios suggest that the current budgetary ceiling may not have to be lifted. They are based on the working assumption that new members will start to join in 2002, and contain a reform of the CAP. Moreover, the 2000 intergovernmental conference will again consider the implications of enlargement for the EU's institutions. The European Union has also struck free trade agreements with Mediterranean countries, which provide for free trade in industrial goods, but are less ambitious otherwise than the agreements with the eastern European countries. On the other hand, the Customs Union Agreement between the European Union and Turkey entered into force in 1996 and fairly ambitious free trade agreements with Mexico and South Africa were signed recently.

Trade across the Atlantic could still benefit from deeper integration

The New Transatlantic Agenda includes many initiatives to eliminate trade barriers that hinder trade across the Atlantic. It does accelerate trade liberalisation beyond that which can be achieved at the multilateral level, for instance via a Mutual Recognition Agreement and co-operation in customs and competition matters. However, it does not provide for the creation of a free trade area, even though the Commission recently launched an initiative to broaden the trade agenda significantly.

The European Union is pushing for a rapid preparation of another trade liberalisation round

Concerning the multilateral agenda, the European Union played a major role in the recently negotiated agreements on information technology, basic telecommunications and financial services liberalisation. However, it is not in favour of a sectoral liberalisation approach but prefers a global approach, which should make it easier for all participants in trade negotiations to share in the mutual benefits from comprehensive and broad liberalisation. After the failure to launch a new round of trade liberalisation in Seattle, the European Union is pushing for the rapid preparation of another round. The European Union also supports an early start to negotiations in the WTO on multilateral rules for international investment and competition policy which have become increasingly important in underpinning effective market access in an increasingly integrated world.

Environmental and labour issues have come to the fore

On environmental issues, the European Union had ambitious goals for the work of the WTO's Committee on Trade and Environment, but its wide-ranging agenda ran into considerable opposition by other countries. However, the European Union is still convinced that trade and the environment are central aspects of the wider goal of sustainable development on a global basis. Concerning labour standards, on the other hand, the European Union agrees that comparative advantage, particularly of low-wage countries, should not be put into question, but that core labour standards should be promoted. The European Union actually does this by its GSP grading system. Clearly, connecting trade, environment and labour issues moves the agenda considerably beyond the already complex economics of trade liberalisation.

Overall, the Union's track record is encouraging

Overall, the Union's track record in the international trade and investment area is encouraging, but the Union itself could, for instance, still gain considerably from freeing up trade in agriculture and textiles. Globalisation also implies that cross-jurisdictional spillovers will become more serious. The World Trade Organisation is tackling many trade-related issues for which the Union has found practical solutions and the EU's experience shows that deep integration is possible. However, building a global club, whose governance structure is accepted by all participants, will probably be a long process as economic structures, laws and institutions are diverse and free-riding a temptation. "Walking on more than one leg" might also be fruitful in these areas for finding mutually acceptable solutions and for providing domino effects to free up trade elsewhere.

I. Progress towards freer trade: an overview

Since its creation the European Union has pursued trade liberalisation, by reducing trade barriers internally, by widening the Community, by striking regional trade agreements, and by participating actively in multilateral trade liberalisation efforts.

Internal integration improves access of third countries

The single market, largely accomplished in 1993, stands out as the deepest regional integration scheme worldwide. A first major step towards liberalisation was achieved with the Customs Union formed in 1968. However, non-tariff trade barriers remained and the impetus towards effective implementation of the four freedoms (free movement of goods, services, capital and people) lost momentum. With growth slowing in the mid-1970s, recourse to non-tariff trade barriers and subsidies to protect non-viable industries multiplied. Restrictions concerning services, which should have been progressively abolished, were either only partially eliminated or completely excluded from the liberalisation process.

During the early 1980s, the case for the growth-enhancing effects of liberalisation became widely accepted and the Single Act, containing some 300 proposals for implementing the internal market was ratified in January 1987.[1] The single market goes considerably beyond a customs union as it provides for the abolition of non-tariff barriers and for free factor movement. It is also more ambitious than free trade agreements such as the North American Free Trade Agreement (NAFTA), which abolishes tariffs and quotas among member countries, allowing each country to protect itself against non-Member countries on an individual basis. Another distinguishing feature of the EU scheme is that it provides for EU-wide legislation across a specific range of competencies. Legislation is interpreted and applied by a Court of Justice. Finally, better EU-wide co-ordination of policies was achieved by the signing of the Maastricht Treaty in 1992 and the Amsterdam Treaty in 1997, the former aiming largely at establishing an Economic and Monetary Union (EMU) and the latter at achieving stronger political integration in a number of areas. Table 1 highlights the major differences between the NAFTA and the European Union.

Table 1. **The European Union and NAFTA trade frameworks: an overview**

	European Union	NAFTA
Goods	Since 1992, intra-area trade is free of tariffs and quantitative restrictions.	Five to ten-year phase-out of all tariffs (15 years in sensitive sectors). Liberalisation of NTBs. Elimination of tariffs and quotas on textiles, apparel and cars. Free trade in agricultural products within fifteen years.
Investment	All restrictions have been lifted from the movement of portfolio capital among members. Provisions have been made for firms' freedom of establishment.	National treatment of investors. Mexican export performance, local content, and foreign exchange requirements are being phased out. Reduction of taxes on dividends, interest and royalties. Some restrictions remain in Mexico's basic energy and railroad industries, Canada's cultural industries and US airline and radio industries.
Services	Trade barriers have been removed with the exception of energy, telecommunications and transportation which have undergone liberalisation to varying degrees. Exceptions are also made for leasing services, legal services, accountancy and postal services.	Substantially opens up financial services in Mexico to US and Canada by 2000 (includes phased reduction of tariffs and NTBs in banking, insurance and brokerage sectors). Nearly full liberalisation of telecommunication and land transportation services. Establishment of negative list of exceptions.
Labour	Labour movement is almost completely liberalised. Some barriers still exist in the form of professional and vocational qualifications and limited portability of fringe benefits, pensions, etc.	Includes provisions for entry of business and professional personnel. Intra-company transferees are allowed to enter member countries. 5 500 additional Mexican professionals are allowed to enter the US annually (above global immigration limits).
Antidumping provisions (versus competition policy)	Antidumping measures were eliminated within the area but common anti-dumping policy exists. Establishment of strong competition policy and enforcement mechanisms covering trade among members.	Continued application of anti-dumping laws but Mexican procedures have been brought closer to those of the US and Canada.
Subsidies	European competition policies have reduced state aid but level of subsidisation is still high. Community-wide subsidy for agricultural products persists (CAP).	No progress made in eliminating subsidies.

Table 1. **The European Union and NAFTA trade frameworks: an overview** *(cont.)*

	European Union	NAFTA
Regulations and standards	Mutual recognition of each country's regulations and standards (includes firms' rights of establishment and certification of professionals) unless minimum community-wide standards have been set (in health, safety, environment). Customs formalities abolished. Some differences in technical standards and indirect taxation persist. Working on harmonisation of technical product standards.	No common set of rules or institutional harmonisation. Enforcement of domestic laws is subject to international scrutiny.
Government procurement	Public procurement of goods and services has been made subject to rules providing for transparency and free market access. Some monitoring problems exist.	Liberalisation of procurement by major government agencies in all three countries.
Dispute settlement	Disputes are handled by the Court of Justice.	Disputes handled by Free Trade Commission (augments dispute settlement provisions of CUSFTA – the Canada-US Free Trade Agreement).
Supranational institutions	Commission (administrative and technical body); Council of Ministers (main decision making body); Court of Justice (enforcement of common body of law); and the Assembly (parliament). Each of these organisations has power that is comparable to institutions in federal states.	Free Trade Commission (supervises implementation of agreement, resolves disputes); Commission for Environmental Cooperation (commits members to improve and enforce domestic environmental protection laws); Commission for Labor Cooperation (forum for consultation on domestic Labor standards). In addition, eight committees and six working groups on various trade issues.

Source: Adapted from Lawrence (1996).

At the same time the Union has widened beyond the six founding members, with the accessions of the United Kingdom, Denmark and Ireland in 1973, Greece in 1981, Portugal and Spain in 1986 and of Austria, Finland and Sweden in 1995. The Treaty of Rome allows other European nations to join if the existing members unanimously agree and the new members undertake the full duties of membership, which implies enacting the *acquis communautaire*. Today, the European Union is the largest integrated economic area in terms of population in the OECD. GDP is close to that of the United States, and nearly three times larger than that of Japan (Table 2) and its economic weight is likely to grow further with the accession of several central and eastern European countries, Cyprus, Malta and Turkey. In addition, the European Union has become the world's largest trading area, even when excluding intra-EU trade; and foreign direct investment inflows and outflows are only higher in North America.

The implementation of the internal market programme also changed the conditions under which third countries gain access to the Union's markets. Before its implementation, there existed a large number of formal and informal national trade restrictions (Stevens and Young, 1996). Major impediments to access included: national quantitative restrictions,[2] technical barriers to trade, barriers to establishment and the provision of services, restrictions due to company law, taxation and intellectual and industrial property rights, barriers due to restrictive public procurement regimes, and access restrictions in heavily regulated industries.

Table 2. **Economic indicators: an international comparison**

	North America[1]	Japan	EU15
Population			
1998, million	300.5	126.5	375.5
GDP			
1998, billion US$			
1995 PPP rates	9 517	2 933	8 260
Exchange rates	9 364	3 809	8 503
Real GDP			
Average growth 1993-98, per cent	3.5	1.2	2.4
Trade in total goods[2]			
Per cent of GDP, average 1993-98			
Trade share	7.0	8.0	9.0
Trade balance	–2.5	2.3	0.2
International direct investment flows[2]			
Average 1993-98, billion US$			
Inflows	82.8	1.3	45.5
Outflows	91.5	21.4	78.9

1. Canada and the United States.
2. Excluding intra-zone trade.
Source: OECD.

While in some of these areas barriers have come down considerably or been eliminated entirely, others continue to hamper trade internally and externally.

Table 3 provides a qualitative overview of the earlier restrictions *vis-à-vis* non-Member countries and the direction of change in the implementation of such restrictions. The entries in the table suggest that access has improved considerably. For instance, internal border controls have been suppressed for European Union as well as for non-EU firms and much fewer quantitative import restrictions exist now. Other changes, such as the removal of barriers concerning services, were a mixture of harmonisation and liberalisation, from which non-EU suppliers have benefited to varying degrees.

It is impossible to evaluate in full the scale, incidence and effects of previously existing restrictions. However, data on quantitative restrictions, public procurement and changes in regulated industries, such as energy and telecommunications contain useful information.[3] While data on the actual use of quantitative import restrictions and informal arrangements restricting imports are not complete, the applications by Member States to implement national level import restrictions (under Article 115) provide a helpful barometer of the changes in trade regimes at the national level. Restrictions rose sharply in the early 1970s (about 50 applications per year) to a peak of more than 350 applications in the early 1980s and subsided afterwards with a steep decline in the early 1990s. While applications in the early 1990s were very few, in 1992 some 6 421 national quantitative restrictions existed concerning products imported from non-state trading countries.[4] Countries concerned were mainly Asian and three-quarters of the products belonged to the textile and clothing sectors. In addition, 4 800 quantitative restrictions covered products from state trading countries, the principal target being China.[5] Finally, bilateral industry-to-industry and other import-limiting arrangements existed. While national quantitative restrictions under Article 115 have been removed,[6] some have been replaced by Community-wide restrictions. The latter mainly concern textile and clothing products and imports from China. In the case of replacement of national by EU-wide quotas, third party effects depend on the extent to which countries were favoured or hurt by the old regime. Beyond national Article 115 restrictions, a few bilateral export monitoring and restraint arrangements have continued at the EU-level after 1993, the most prominent being the 1991 "consensus" on cars with Japan. The voluntary export restraint agreement concerning Japanese car imports expired at the end of 1999.

Another area where at least some quantification is possible is public procurement. Traditionally, public procurement markets were among the most sheltered, and according to the Cecchini Report, they were characterised in 1987 by nationalistic purchasing, lack of transparency, wide price differences for similar products and negligible cross-border trade. The original Works and Supplies Directives of 1971 and 1977, and the 1979 Tokyo Round Government Procurement

Table 3. **The effect of internal market changes on third parties**

Pre-IMP[1] barrier	External effect	Nature of change	Potential external effect of change
Quantitative restrictions (QR) in Member States	Discrimination between internal and external	Removal of QRs	Better access for externals
		Substitution of EC QRs	Complex change
	Discrimination among third parties	Removal of QRs	Better access for some; more competition for others
		Substitution of EC QRs	Complex change
Physical barriers between Member States (*e.g.* controls on borders)	No differential effects *vis-à-vis* domestic suppliers	Removal of barriers	Increased ease of supply
Technical barriers (*e.g.* regulations and standards)	No differential effects	Mutual recognition	Access to new markets, more competition in old markets
		Harmonisation	Complex change
	Discrimination among third parties (*e.g.* MRAs)	Mutual recognition	Access to new markets, more competition in old markets
		Harmonisation	Complex change
Barriers to provision of services, right of establishment and free movement of capital (*e.g.* financial services, transport)	No differential effect	Primarily liberalisation	Greater ease of establishment
Barriers in the business environment (*e.g.* intellectual and industrial property, company law, taxation and media)	No differential effect	Primarily approximation	Simpler operating conditions
Public procurement	No differential effect	Some liberalisation	Mix of opening plus continued discrimination
Barriers in regulated industries (*e.g.* energy and telecommunications)	No differential effect	Primarily liberalisation	Improved access

1. IMP: Internal Market Programme.
Source: Stevens and Young (1996).

Agreement had done little to change the situation. The internal market programme introduced new legislation on regulating works, supply and services contracts of public bodies and a separate Directive on purchases by utilities, whether publicly owned or not.[7] By opening the tendering to non-national companies the Directives gave new opportunities to firms from third countries, even though non-EU firms face some discrimination in the utilities sector, if no bilateral agreement exists. While the public procurement market is fairly large (close to 14 per cent of GDP in 1998), published public procurement contracts had a value of a little less than 2 per cent of GDP. Moreover, imports of such goods are still fairly low. Commission data for 1998 indicate that the share of procurement imports in total imports were below 10 per cent for Germany, Spain and Italy but above 25 per cent for Greece, Denmark and Finland, and above 30 per cent for Ireland.

While the single market has led to deep integration over a wide range of sectors and also benefited non-EU member countries, the first large-scale assessment of the Commission (European Commission, 1996*a*) pointed to the need to be vigilant against backsliding and to pursue integration further, for instance, in public procurement, company law and taxation.[8] The Commission's attention has now turned to the enforcement of the single market (in early 2000 around 10 per cent of the single market directives were still not implemented), to the monitoring of market developments and to reaping synergies with other policy areas. With the 1997 Action Plan for the Single Market, the Commission stepped up efforts to monitor progress. It also submitted a progress report on the functioning of product and capital markets to the Council, which forms part of the so-called Cardiff process. Sectoral policy frameworks have also been developed, for instance, for public procurement and financial services. While the single market agenda will be developed further (e-commerce, taxation issues), the Commission also aims at a better integration between EU-wide and national policies, by further developing the examination of Member countries' product market policies in the Internal Market Council into a peer review exercise.

An expanding network of regional trade arrangements

While there were many proposals and attempts to form free trade agreements or customs unions during the 1960s, regional integration schemes played little role up to the end of the decade, except for the European Community, the European Free Trade Association (EFTA) and the now defunct Council of Mutual Economic Assistance.[9] However, regional integration schemes have started to flourish again outside Europe since the early 1980s. They include, for instance, the Australia-New Zealand (1983) and the North American Free Trade Agreement (1994) including Canada, the United States and Mexico. In recent years, the number of free trade agreements and customs unions has risen considerably, the European Union and other European countries being especially active. Between 1948 and 1994, GATT contracting parties notified 118 regional trade agreements relating to goods, of which 38 in the five years ending in 1994. Since the creation of the WTO in 1995, 80 additional regional trade agreements covering trade in goods and services have been notified. At the end of 1999, 198 regional trade agreements had been notified to the GATT/WTO, of which 119 are still in force. Virtually all WTO member countries are now party to at least one preferential trade agreement – Japan, the Republic of Korea, Hong Kong (China), China and Mongolia being exceptions. The Community has been a pioneer in entering preferential trading relations. Today, virtually all WTO member countries are covered by reciprocal or non-reciprocal contractual concessions with the European Union, except the United States, Canada, Japan, Australia, New Zealand, Hong Kong (China), China, the Republic of Korea and Singapore. Most of the rise in regional agreements is accounted for by free trade areas, while the Union itself started as a customs union and moved further on to an economic union, which provides for much deeper integration. Countries acceding to the Union have to sign up to the obligations of being a member of the economic union.

With the accession of the United Kingdom, Denmark and Ireland in 1973 a Community-wide policy with respect to the remaining EFTA countries was elaborated and individual free trade agreements for industrial products were signed with the remaining EFTA countries. The outcome of these agreements was the establishment in 1973 of the largest free trade area in the world. Free trade agreements also preceded accession to the European Union for Greece and Spain. Co-operation with the remaining EFTA countries deepened further in the early 1990s, with the establishment of the European Economic Area (EEA), which provided for the implementation of most single market legislation and led to the accessions of Austria, Sweden and Finland in 1995. The EEA applies currently to Norway, Iceland and Liechtenstein. While the Swiss voted to stay out of the EEA in 1992, a trade agreement covering liberalisation measures for several sectors will come into force in 2001. Finally, a customs union between the European Union and Turkey came into force in 1996 (Table 4).

Trade preferences have also played an important role in shaping the trade relations of the former colonies of Member States. With the Yaoundé Convention of 1963 the EEC countries "inherited" the trade preferences provided by France and Belgium to their former colonies.[10] It linked the EEC with 18 African States and Madagascar in a series of bilateral free trade agreements. The same question arose again with the accession of the United Kingdom, and the Community established trade relations with the Commonwealth countries. The ACP-EEC Lomé Convention (1975) grouped together the African, Caribbean and Pacific countries (ACP) of the Commonwealth and the Yaoundé countries. Seventy ACP countries were covered by the Fourth Lomé Convention. The Lomé Conventions eliminated duties and other restrictions on most products, except for agricultural products falling under the Common Agricultural Policy and a range of textile and clothing products. The Lomé Convention expired in February 2000 (see below). Like the other WTO members the European Union extends non-reciprocal trade

Table 4. **The network of regional agreements**

Main agreements notified to the GATT/WTO[1]

Area	Agreement
European Union	Treaty of Rome establishing the European Communities European Free Trade Association (EFTA) European Economic Area (EEA) Europe Agreements with central and eastern European countries Partnership and Co-operation Agreements with NIS Partnership Agreement of Suva with African, Caribbean and Pacific (ACP) States Interregional Framework Partnership Agreement Customs unions (Andorra, Malta, San Marino, Turkey) Free Trade Agreements or areas (Cyprus, Faroe Islands, Mexico, South Africa, Switzerland) EEC-Association of certain non-European countries and territories (EEC-PTOM II) Euro-Mediterranean Association (Israel, Jordan, Morocco, PLO, Tunisia) Co-operation Agreements (Algeria, Egypt, Lebanon, Syria)
Central and eastern European countries and NIS	Central European Free Trade Area (CEFTA) Customs union (Belarus, Kazakhstan, Kyrgyz Republic, Russian Federation) Free Trade Agreement (Estonia, Latvia, Lithuania) Trade Agreements between NIS Numerous bilateral and multilateral agreements within the area
EFTA and other European countries	European Free Trade Association (EFTA) EFTA Free Trade Agreements with central and eastern European countries Bilateral agreements between Turkey and central and eastern European countries
North America	North American Free Trade Association (NAFTA) Israel-United States bilateral agreement Canada-Israel and Canada-Chile bilateral agreements
Latin America and Caribbean	Central American Common Market (CACM) Caribbean Community and Common Market (CARICOM) Latin American Integration Association (LAIA)[2] Southern Common Market (MERCOSUR)[2] Andean Group[2]
Asia and Oceania	Australia-New Zealand Closer Economic Relations Trade Agreement (ANZCERTA) South Asian Preferential Trade Arrangement (SAPTA)[2] Bangkok Agreement[2] Common Effective Preferential Tariff (CEPT) Scheme for ASEAN Free Trade Area[2] South Pacific Regional Trade and Economic Co-operation Agreement (SPARTECA)[2] Melanesian Spearhead Group[2]
Africa	Southern African Customs Union (SACU) Common Market for eastern and southern Africa (COMESA)[2] West African Economic and Monetary Union (UEMOA)[2]

Table 4. **The network of regional agreements** *(cont.)*

Main agreements notified to the GATT/WTO[1]

Area	Agreement
Middle East	Unified Economic Agreement among member states of the Gulf Co-operation Council (GCC)[2] Preferential Tariffs among members of the Economic Co-operation Organisation (ECO)
Other[2]	Protocol relating to Trade Negotiations among Developing Countries Global System of Trade Prefereences (GSTP)

1. In force in May 2000 except for certain agreements noted otherwise.
2. In force in January 2000.

Source: WTO, May 2000.

preferences under the Generalised System of Preferences (GSP) to a large number of developing countries outside the Lomé Convention.[11]

When the EC formulated its policy towards the ACP countries, it also developed a "Mediterranean policy", covering trade relations with Turkey, the former Yugoslavia, the Maghreb (Algeria, Tunisia and Morocco), the Mashreq countries (Egypt, Jordan, Lebanon, Syria) and Israel. These agreements differed in the treatment of products imported from the EC and in the speed of elimination of trade barriers. Recently, a new initiative concerning the Mediterranean countries outside the European Union was taken to speed up co-operation (see below).

Trade relations within Europe changed profoundly with the transition of the former centrally planned economies to market economies. The starting point of deepening trade relations were the Europe Agreements with the Czech and Slovak Republic, Hungary and Poland in 1991 and with Bulgaria and Romania in 1993. These treaties recognise the aspirations of these countries to future EU membership and provide for the establishment of free trade agreements in the interim, with certain sensitive sectors being covered by protocols. The agreements also include provisions on rules of origin, competition policy, etc. In 1994, the European Union signed free trade agreements with the Baltic states. Currently, accession of ten central and eastern European countries is being considered. Except for the Baltic states, co-operation with the former Soviet states is still in its infancy.

The result of the post-war process of regional integration is the creation of different levels of trade liberalisation. The deepest level of integration applies to the European Union itself, but most of this extends to the other west European countries through the EEA. A second circle is formed of the central and eastern European countries, as well as those Mediterranean countries with whom reciprocal trade agreements have been concluded. Some of these agreements are a first step towards future accession. A third circle is formed by the non-reciprocal agreements with the north African and ACP countries.

Reaping the gains from freer trade was clearly not the sole impetus – and often not the major reason – motivating negotiations of trade agreements and thus distinguishes the EU's pursuit of regional agreements from those elsewhere. Historically, in the early EFTA agreements and first generation agreements with the Mediterranean countries, preferential agreements for trade liberalisation provided an economic dimension to wider agreements with neighbouring countries; and the Lomé Conventions are seen to provide an economic underpinning to support economic, social and political reforms in these countries. Similarly, the preferential agreements with the central and eastern European countries were seen as the first step towards Community membership. The set of overall objectives pursued goes significantly beyond the provision of a close and stable economic relationship and often covers also technical and administrative assistance. Frequently, considerable amounts of financial assistance flow from the European Union to the partner countries (European Commission, 1993). Clearly, being surrounded by peaceful and prosperous regions is very important for the well-being of the Community itself.

EU agreements and unilateral concessions now cover virtually all countries in the world, major trading partners, such as the United States, Japan and Canada being exceptions. The number of such agreements has risen considerably since the early days of the Community. For instance, regional trade arrangements covered only 27 countries in 1970 but now cover close to 100, with another 40 countries receiving unilateral concessions under the Generalised System of Preferences. This could suggest that virtually all trade is on a preferential basis. However, the geographic coverage exaggerates the importance of regional agreements for trade as the share of extra-EU imports from countries receiving Most Favoured Nation (MFN) treatment is close to a third, largely reflecting the high degree of trade integration among the European Union and the non-European OECD countries and the size of these markets. The Community import share originating both from countries covered by reciprocal trade agreements and by unilateral concessions is also close to a third. In addition, the overall share of imports entering on a non-discriminatory basis is larger than a third due to the fact that more than 30 per cent of EU imports enter duty free, in which case trade preferences do not represent a benefit for the preferred country (Sapir, 1998). Including intra-area trade, Grether and Olarreaga (1998) calculated an EU15 share of preferential trade in total trade of 70 per cent for 1993-97 as compared to 28 per cent for the NAFTA and 18 per cent for the MERCOSUR (Southern Common Market). It was only 3 per cent in the Asia-Oceania region.

While geographic and trade coverage can be measured, it is not possible to measure the degree of trade liberalisation among members of the regional trade arrangements as no comprehensive measures of national trade barriers exist. While the OECD, for instance, produces data on overall support levels for agriculture or tariff and non-tariff barriers for trade in goods, these data do not allow the measurement of the margins of preference of regional trade arrangements. It is clear, on the other hand, that the sectoral coverage of the agreements has increased; margins of preference have fallen with multilateral liberalisation; non-tariff barriers have also been reduced; and agreements leading up to EU membership, such as the EEA and Europe Agreements, provide for deep integration.

Multilateral liberalisation has kept momentum

Regional trade integration has gone hand in hand with significant multilateral trade liberalisation under the auspices of the GATT and the WTO. Multilateral trade policy is, in principle, a competence of the Community and guided by the Treaties. They provide for a complex interplay between the Council, the Commission and the Parliament, while in a number of areas trade competencies are shared between the Community and the Member countries. The institutional framework is outlined in Annex I.

Progress towards liberalising trade in a worldwide context has shown unsteady yet distinct momentum over the last decades. At the time of its creation, EEC average tariff rates for manufactured goods differed sharply, ranging from 6.4 per cent for Germany to 18.7 per cent for Italy in 1958 (Table 5). Rates fell somewhat after the Dillon Round in 1961 and more so for the countries with high tariff rates. With the introduction of the common external tariff the average tariff rate was 10.4 per cent in 1968, implying sharp falls in tariff protection for Italy and France, a considerable increase for Germany and to a lesser extent, increases for the Benelux countries. After the five-year phasing in of the 1968 Kennedy Round, the average tariff fell to 6.6 per cent. Overall, tariff protection declined considerably between 1958 and the early 1970s. Over the same period, tariff protection was relatively low in Denmark and Sweden, but fairly high in the United Kingdom, Austria, Finland and Norway.[12]

Contrary to developments in manufacturing, the introduction of the Common Agricultural Policy (CAP) during the 1960s[13] led to rising protection in the agricultural sector. Calculations by Thorbecke and Pagoulatos (1975) show that *ad valorem* tariff equivalents of pre-CAP import restrictions were for most agricultural products far higher than tariff rates for manufactured products and that they increased considerably until the end of the 1960s. In the United Kingdom, Ireland and Denmark levels of agricultural protection, while also sizeable, were significantly lower. In addition, the 1962 Long-Term Arrangement Regarding Trade in Cotton Textiles (the forerunner to the Multifiber Agreement) led to a highly protectionist system of trade in textiles, which was little changed by the Kennedy Round.

Table 5. **Multilateral tariff reductions**

Simple average MFN tariff rates, industrial products

	1958	After Dillon Round	1968 External tariff	After Kennedy Round
Belgium	9.7	8.7		
France	17.0	15.3		
Germany	6.4	5.8	10.4	6.6
Italy	18.7	16.8		
Netherlands	9.7	8.7		
United Kingdom	16.5	14.9	14.9	9.2
Denmark	5.6	5.2	5.2	3.2
Austria	14.9	11.4	11.4	8.2
Sweden	6.5	6.3	6.3	4.2
Norway	10.3	10.3	10.3	6.4

Source: Resnick and Truman (1975).

Progress towards multilateral liberalisation was slow during the early 1970s and the significant resurgence of protectionist pressures, especially via non-tariff measures, showed the necessity to enlarge the mandate of the GATT or to make existing rules operational. Negotiations of the Tokyo Round started in 1973. It was far more ambitious in its scope, coverage and complexity than the earlier Rounds, which had mainly focused on tariff reductions. Negotiations focused on many new areas, for instance, the elimination of quantitative restrictions and technical barriers to trade, subsidies and countervailing duties; government procurement and agricultural liberalisation also received strong attention.[14]

The Tokyo Round led to a reduction in the external EC tariff levels by some 3 percentage points to reach 6 per cent and rate dispersion was reduced considerably. While the agreement focused on greater clarity, precision and enlarged coverage of provisions concerning subsidies, countervailing duties or public procurement rules, these had only minor overall effects. For instance, while subsidies in the European Union have come down since the mid-1980s, they still remain high in international comparison (Figure 1) and trade in publicly procured goods has only started to rise in recent years from very low levels. In addition, little progress was made on agricultural trade, and levels of protection, as measured by Producer Support Estimates, remained very high (Figure 2). Indeed, among the large agricultural producers very high levels of protection persisted only in Japan and the European Union, while they declined considerably in the United States since the mid-1980s and later on in Canada; and protection was always low in Australia. Finally, the Round made no headway in reining in the use of non-tariff measures, such as anti-dumping actions (Figure 3), voluntary export restraint and orderly marketing arrangements.

Figure 1. **Subsidisation**

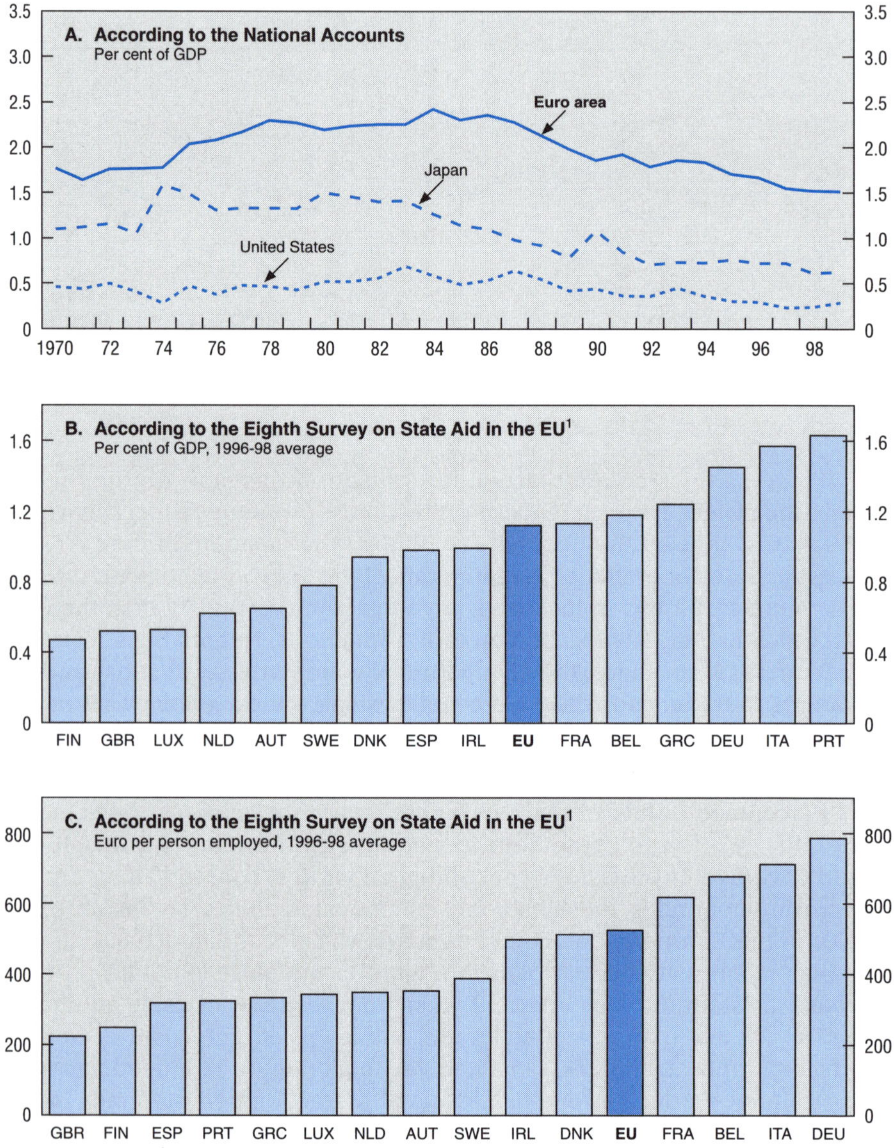

1. Overall national aid excluding agriculture. Aid includes direct grants, tax reductions, equity participations and aid elements contained in soft loans, tax deferrals and State guarantees but excludes EU subsidies.

Source: OECD, *National Accounts* and European Commission (2000), *Eighth Survey on State Aid in the European Union.*

Figure 2. **Protection of the agricultural sector**
Producer support estimates (PSE), per cent[1]

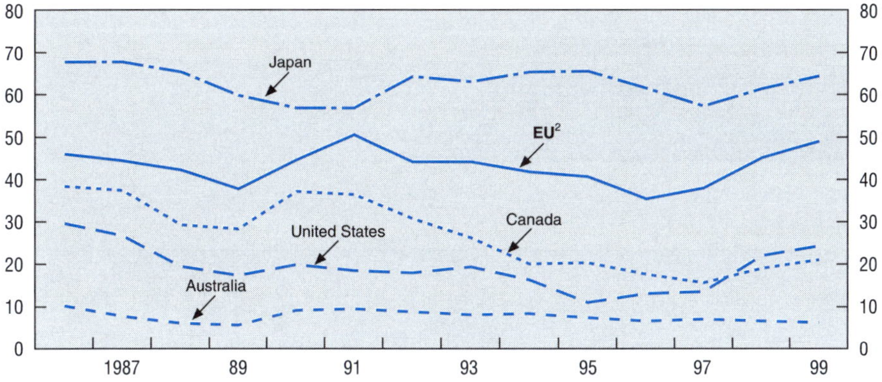

1. The percentage PSE is the annual monetary value of gross transfers from consumers and taxpayers to agricultural producers (measured at farm gate level) as a per cent of the value of total gross farm receipts, measured by the value of total production (at farm gate prices), plus budgetary support.
2. EU12 for 1986-94 and EU15 from 1995 onwards. EU includes ex-GDR from 1990.

Source: OECD (2000), *Agricultural Policies in OECD Countries. Monitoring and Evaluation.*

The goals set for the Uruguay Round were even more ambitious than those for the Tokyo Round. Apart from cutting tariffs further, efforts were made to broaden the world trading system to include services and intellectual property rights, and to achieve a full return of agriculture, textiles and clothing to the system. As a result of the Round, most industrial tariffs will fall below 5 per cent in the developed countries, while the Agreement on Textiles and Clothing requires a gradual phase out of the Multifiber Arrangement (MFA) quota restrictions over a ten year transition period. Concerning agriculture, the Round provided for the conversion of non-tariff barriers to tariffs, the reduction of tariffs and export subsidies, and disciplines on domestic support. Where market access was largely absent, countries have to provide for a minimum 3 per cent import share of domestic output at the outset, rising to 5 per cent over the implementation period of six years, at "low or minimal" tariff rates. Also "grey area" measures, such as voluntary export restraints and orderly marketing arrangements, have been prohibited.

New issues covered in this Round concerned intellectual property rights, trade-related investment measures, and trade in services. Concerning the latter, the General Agreement on Trade in Services provides a framework for liberalising services across borders (services supplied from one country to another), consumption abroad, commercial presence and the temporary presence of persons to

Figure 3. **Number of outstanding antidumping actions**
1981-99[1]

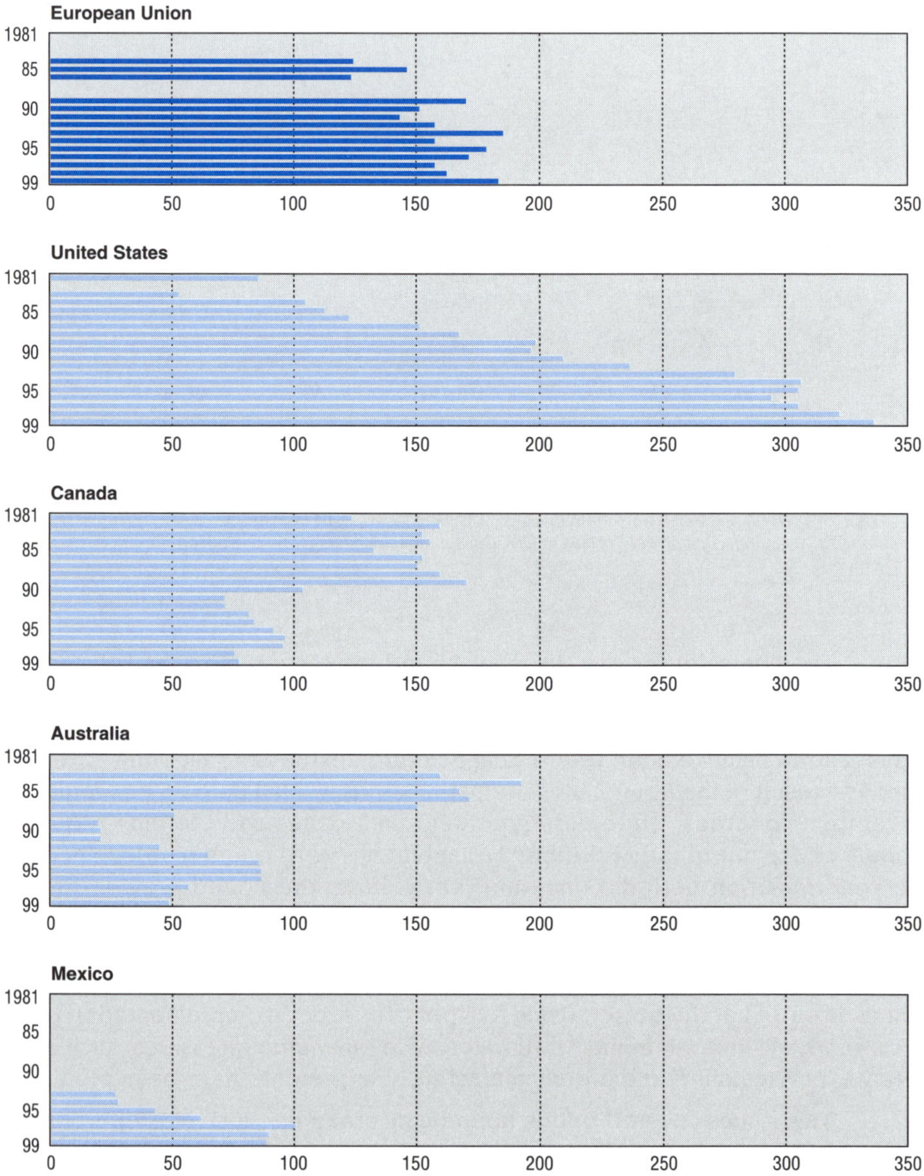

1. At 30th June.
Source: WTO and GATT.

deliver services. As for goods, a cornerstone of the agreement is the unconditional MFN principle, even though exemptions from this principle have been granted for specific periods, which cannot be extended.

Foreign direct investment has become an important market access strategy due to the continued growth of foreign trade, liberalisation of national markets and the rapid integration of financial markets. The rise in foreign direct investment has been impressive since the early 1980s the European Union being the second largest host and source area of foreign direct investment globally after North America. Yet, trade-related investment measures were only included explicitly at the Uruguay Round. However, given the rising importance of foreign direct investment and multinational enterprises, bilateral treaties have proliferated as well as regional and other multilateral agreements. Concerning the latter, the most active fora have been the OECD and the World Bank (Witherell, 1996).

Furthermore, the Uruguay Round managed to strengthen multilateral disciplines by clarifying concepts and agreeing on new understandings of safeguards, anti-dumping, subsidies, countervailing duties, etc. and by strengthening the dispute settlement system significantly. Finally, a main feature of the Round was the creation of the World Trade Organisation, where membership is conditional on countries having schedules of concessions and commitments on market access in agricultural, industrial and service sectors. Membership also implies acceptance of the GATT's *acquis* until 1994 and the Uruguay Round agreements. A recent OECD exercise that has measured regulatory intensity for inward and outward oriented regulatory activities suggests that the multilateral liberalisation efforts and disciplines have led to trade regimes which are much more similar across countries than are inward oriented regulatory regimes (Nicoletti *et al.*, 1999).

Contrary to earlier agreements, the economic effects of the Uruguay Round have been well researched. A summary of this research is provided in Box 1.

Box 1. Quantitative assessments of the Uruguay Round

There is a sizeable empirical literature assessing the Uruguay Round Agreements. These quantitative studies, based on computable general equilibrium (CGE) models, generally conclude that countries that liberalise the most tend to gain the most. CGE studies generally cover tariff cuts, the phasing out of the MFA and other industrial quantitative restrictions, and liberalisation in agriculture. What is generally taken as constant or ignored in the modelling, however, is the use of contingent protection as well as the impact of liberalisation in the service sector.

All these models emphasise the impact of trade liberalisation on resource allocation, directly through efficiency gains, while some others provide for an indirect link through income-induced changes in capital accumulation rates. The main differences in the models' structure can be pinned down to: *i)* the level of sectoral and regional aggregation, *ii)* different assumptions on market structure, and *iii)* the inclusion or disregard of accumulation effects.

Francois et al. (1996), after having controlled for differences in the liberalisation coverage, differences in models' structure and in the base year used, present comparable estimates from the available post Uruguay Round CGE literature. They find that the regional and sectoral model structure largely determines the relative size of the impact. Models especially designed to study liberalisation in agriculture (*e.g.* the RUNS model of the OECD and the World Bank), and giving less emphasis to the formalisation of the manufacturing sector, will attribute higher gains to agricultural liberalisation. Models incorporating scale economies and imperfect competition deliver stronger gains from liberalisation; and, similarly, the estimation of dynamic gains from capital-induced accumulation effects adds to static efficiency gains. Different assumptions about product markets also influence the results. Models with products originating from different countries that are assumed to be imperfect substitutes within the same product category (the so-called Armington assumption) deliver smaller liberalisation effects than models where products are assumed to be homogenous or differentiated at the firm level.

Overall these studies find that the world as a whole gains from the Uruguay Round (the OECD's estimate pointing to a gain of about 1 per cent of GDP). The gains are concentrated in developed countries, especially the European Union, Japan and the United States. The intuition is that these countries liberalised areas that were very costly in terms of foregone welfare to themselves, most notably by reducing agricultural and MFA protection. However, the gains from reducing agricultural protection are probably considerably overestimated, as most modellers assumed an average reduction in protection of 36 per cent, which is far from being the case for tariffed products. On the other hand, the disregard of service sector liberalisation biases most model results downwards. A notable exception is the study by Brown *et al.* (1995) where gains from services' trade liberalisation are estimated to be larger than those from further liberalisation of trade in goods.

II. The current trade regime in international comparison

Comparisons of trade regimes are difficult as no comprehensive measures of trade policies exist which could be used to simulate a country's distance from an "ideal" world of free trade. In the following, the effects of the Uruguay Round on the EU's current trade regime are outlined and trade policy indicators compared to those of the other Quad countries. Recent developments concerning the EU's regional agreements are covered in the chapter on the EU's future trade agenda as they are currently being shaped or reshaped.

Tariff barriers are losing in importance

As a result of the Uruguay Round, tariffs are increasingly losing importance as trade policy instruments. In addition to an overall increase in bindings, which reduces the use of tariffs as a discriminatory policy instrument, enhanced market access will be ensured by an overall reduction of tariffs of almost 40 per cent. In the European Union, the simple average tariff on manufacturing products has been reduced to 4.2 per cent in 1999 and should decline further to 3.7 per cent in 2000. In non-food manufactured products, where all tariffs are *ad valorem* tariffs, tariff peaks will all be lower than 20 per cent by the year 2001.[15] Moreover, the share of duty-free imports in developed countries will more than double after the implementation of the cuts, rising from 20 to 44 per cent of imports.

While this section focuses on the multilateral trading system, it should be remembered that a distinguishing feature of the EU's trade policy is the extent of preferential agreements. However, while the vast majority of the EU's trading partners qualify for preferential treatment, in terms of value, more than 60 per cent of imports to the Community are not affected by preferential treatment (see above). Also, both the lowering of tariff levels and the increase in the duty-free treatment will lead to a reduction in the importance of preferential trade. In the absence of an up-to-date detailed data set, the following discussion of tariff and non-tariff barriers in international comparison focuses on 1996 data (OECD, 1997*a*). WTO calculations (WTO, 2000*a*) indicate that the EU's MFN applied tariff rate has declined from 9.5 per cent in 1996 to 6.9 per cent in 1999.

Despite average rate reductions and the phasing-out of duties in several sectors, tariffs have remained high for certain manufacturing products[16] and, following "tariffication",[17] high tariffs and tariff peaks have replaced non-tariff barriers in agriculture. OECD (1997*b*) shows that the average tariff reduction rule for agricultural products has been widely used to concentrate tariff reductions in less sensitive product categories, where tariffs were generally already low, and to minimise reductions in sensitive, high tariff, product categories. In the case of the European Union, tariffication resulted in prohibitively high tariffs on dairy products, sugar, fruit and vegetables.

On the basis of duty-free tariff lines and average applied MFN rates, both the use of tariffs[18] and the level of protection seem to be greater in the European Union than in the United States and Japan. Specifically, the import-weighted average tariff rate was 6.6 per cent in the European Union in 1996, as compared with 3.7 per cent in the United States and 3.5 per cent in Japan[19] (Table 6). The use of MFN rates as indicators of overall protection can be misleading in the presence of preferential agreements. In Table 6, MFN applied rates are used instead of collected tariff rates (*i.e.* inclusive of preferential rates). The relevance of the applied MFN tariff rate as an indicator of distortions will depend on the size and elasticity of supply from the countries which benefit from preferential rates. If supply is relatively limited and inelastic, the applied MFN rate might be the relevant marginal rate. In the opposite case the relevant tariff will be lower than the applied MFN tariff depending on the size of imports entitled to preferential treatment (OECD, 1997*a*). Concerning duty free items, it should be noted that the number of duty free lines reported here applies only to products covered by MFN treatment and not to those covered by preferential treatment. The importance of duty-free treatment for the European Union and the United States is thus underestimated with respect to Japan.

The noticeable increase in the EU simple average applied tariff (from 7.6 per cent in 1993 to 9.5 per cent in 1996) reflects the impact of the "tariffication" process in the agricultural sector, which outweighed reductions elsewhere.[20] The EU's relatively high protection levels in the agricultural sector clearly affect comparisons of these indicators. Looking at the production-weighted average tariff rate, for which a disaggregation by sector is available, the average level of protection in the European Union has, in fact, declined from 8.4 per cent in 1993 to 7.7 per cent in 1996 (Table 7). Increases in sectoral rates are in those areas hit by tariffication, agriculture and processed food, while tariffs on textile and apparel products have remained relatively high in all Quad countries, with EU tariffs being the lowest in 1996. On the other hand, tariffs in the other manufacturing sectors have become low in all Quad countries, with tariffs being lowest in Japan, followed by the European Union and the United States, and highest in Canada. The pattern of sectoral protection is similar across the Quad countries.

Table 6. **Structure of applied MFN tariffs in the Quad countries**[1]

Per cent

	United States			European Union[2]		
	1989	1993	1996	1988	1993	1996
1. Bound tariff lines	98.1	98.1	100.0	91.8	92.7	100.0
2. Duty-free tariff lines	17.4	14.4	17.8	10.5	10.9	11.4
3. Specific and compound tariffs/all tariffs	17.6	17.0	17.7	10.6	11.1	12.1
4. Tariff quotas/all tariffs	0.1	0.2	2.3	1.0	2.4	2.3
5. Tariffs with no *ad valorem* equivalent	1.3	1.6	5.7	8.4	8.1	2.0
6. Simple average bound tariff rate[3]	6.3	6.5	3.9	7.5	7.6	7.2
7. Simple average applied tariff rate	6.2	6.4	6.2	7.4	7.6	9.5
8. Import-weighted average tariff rate[4]	4.0	4.0	3.7	6.0	6.2	6.6
9. Production weighted average tariff rate[5]	4.4	4.7	5.2	8.2	8.4	7.7
10. Domestic tariff "spikes"[6]	4.5	4.0	3.8	2.2	2.3	4.8
11. Overall standard deviation (SD)	7.7	8.6	14.2	6.1	6.1	20.7
	Japan			**Canada**		
	1988	1993	1996	1988	1993	1996
1. Bound tariff lines	89.8	90.5	98.8	98.4	98.6	99.6
2. Duty-free tariff lines	21.9	35.4	34.8	25.7	26.3	31.6
3. Specific and compound tariffs/all tariffs	7.4	8.8	10.6	8.6	6.2	9.1
4. Tariff quotas/all tariffs	1.0	1.2	2.2	0.0	0.0	1.5
5. Tariffs with no *ad valorem* equivalent	1.0	0.4	4.0	0.5	0.1	2.5
6. Simple average bound tariff rate[3]	8.2	8.5	4.7	9.3	9.3	5.1
7. Simple average applied tariff rate	6.9	7.0	6.7	9.1	8.8	9.2
8. Import-weighted average tariff rate[4]	3.8	3.6	3.5	6.9	6.7	5.7
9. Production weighted average tariff rate[5]	4.2	3.6	3.4	8.7	8.4	12.1
10. Domestic tariff "spikes"[6]	5.3	5.7	6.8	0.5	0.3	1.4
11. Overall standard deviation (SD)	8.9	12.7	11.8	8.8	8.4	27.5

1. Indicators 7 to 11 include *ad valorem* equivalents (AVEs) for specific and compound duties when available. For 1996, *ad valorem* equivalents were made available only for Canada and the EU. For other countries, AVEs are estimated using AVEs of base rates and Uruguay Round bound rates when available, and interpolating for 1996 rates under the assumption of equal installment in reduction rates from the base to the bound rate. Different durations for reduction for each product have been taken into consideration.
2. Indicators encompass sliding charges.
3. Uruguay Round bound rates aligned to 1996 tariff schedules are available only for the EU. For all other countries, bound rates were provided based on the base year (1988/89) tariff nomenclatures. With the exception of the EU, the average for 1996 is therefore based on those nomenclatures.
4. Constant OECD import weights.
5. For the EU, German weights are used.
6. Domestic tariff "spikes" are defined as those exceeding three times the overall simple average MFN rate.

Source: OECD (1997*a*).

Table 7. **Production-weighted average applied MFN tariff rates in the Quad countries**[1]

Per cent

ISIC code	Industry	United States 1989	United States 1993	United States 1996	European Union 1988	European Union 1993	European Union 1996
1	Agriculture, forestry, fishing	3.8	4.1	7.9	6.4	6.1	10.7
2	Mining and quarrying	0.2	0.2	0.2	0.5	0.3	0.6
21	Coal mining	0.0	0.0	0.0	0.4	0.0	0.0
22	Crude petroleum	0.1	0.1	0.1	..	..	0.9
23	Metal ore mining	1.2	1.2	1.1	..	..	0.0
29	Other mining	1.1	1.1	0.9	1.0	1.0	0.7
3	Manufacturing	4.7	5.0	5.4	8.4	8.6	7.7
31	Food, beverages and tobacco	7.6	8.2	15.9	27.4	27.1	32.5
32	Textiles and apparel	11.6	11.8	11.3	10.0	9.9	9.8
33	Wood and wood products	4.1	4.2	3.5	5.2	5.4	3.4
34	Paper and paper products	2.0	2.0	1.8	7.1	7.2	4.7
35	Chemicals, petroleum products	5.7	5.8	4.4	6.4	6.5	5.3
36	Non-metallic mineral products	4.9	5.0	4.5	5.5	5.4	3.9
37	Basic metal industries	4.1	4.3	3.7	5.1	5.1	3.6
38	Fabricated metal products	3.5	3.9	3.2	6.0	6.3	4.3
39	Other manufacturing	6.0	5.9	4.8	5.6	5.5	4.2
	Total all products	**4.4**	**4.7**	**5.2**	**8.2**	**8.4**	**7.7**
		Japan			**Canada**		
		1988	1993	1996	1988	1993	1996
1	Agriculture, forestry, fishing	5.1	5.1	5.0	4.1	4.0	5.5
2	Mining and quarrying	0.5	0.3	0.3	3.4	3.4	1.9
21	Coal mining	..	..	..	0.0	0.0	0.0
22	Crude petroleum	..	..	..	5.8	5.8	3.8
23	Metal ore mining	..	..	..	0.0	0.0	0.0
29	Other mining	..	..	..	3.2	3.2	0.8
3	Manufacturing	4.1	3.5	3.3	10.0	9.7	14.4
31	Food, beverages and tobacco	15.6	17.5	18.9	16.8	15.6	57.4
32	Textiles and apparel	10.4	11.7	10.1	20.2	19.6	17.8
33	Wood and wood products	5.0	3.7	3.6	9.0	8.9	6.7
34	Paper and paper products	2.0	1.6	1.2	6.3	6.4	3.8
35	Chemicals, petroleum products	4.6	4.3	3.2	9.6	9.4	6.3
36	Non-metallic mineral products	2.9	1.7	1.5	6.9	6.7	4.3
37	Basic metal industries	4.1	3.7	3.0	6.9	6.8	4.1
38	Fabricated metal products	1.7	0.3	0.3	7.3	7.2	5.0
39	Other manufacturing	3.8	2.9	2.5	10.9	10.1	6.8
	Total all products	**4.2**	**3.6**	**3.4**	**8.7**	**8.4**	**12.1**

1. Based on each country's own value-added.

Source: OECD.

The use of specific tariffs has increased due to the process of tariffication. In this respect, the United States was ranked first in 1996, with such tariffs amounting to 17.7 per cent of all tariffs, as compared with 12.1 per cent for the European Union, and 10.6 per cent for Japan. Overall, the "tariffication" process leads to an increase in the "quantified" average tariff level, to higher levels of distortion in the tariff structure and to a reduction in tariff "escalation".

While the United States and Japan presented lower levels of overall tariff protection, their tariff structures were more distorting than that of the European Union in 1993. In 1996, tariff dispersion,[21] as measured by the overall standard deviation, increased in most countries due to tariffication of agricultural imports. This trend was more accentuated in the European Union which, in 1996, presented a more distorted tariff schedule than that of the United States or Japan. The standard deviation reached 20.7 per cent in the European Union as compared to 14.2 per cent in the United States and 11.8 per cent in Japan.[22] This is in line with the increase in tariff spikes[23] in the European Union from 2.3 to 4.8 per cent. Abstracting from "tariffication", the tariff schedule in all countries has become less distorting, as high tariffs were cut more than lower ones.

Tariff "escalation" has been another traditional feature displayed by the Community's tariff schedule. Tariff "escalation" takes place when the level of effective protection increases as goods undergo further processing. Tariff escalation in developed countries is of great concern to developing countries, as higher rates of effective protection of processed goods in developed countries could hurt their potential to develop processing industries. The figures in Table 8 give a broad indication of the direction of change in tariff escalation. One should be cautious in drawing conclusions from these figures since the concept of tariff escalation refers to precisely defined manufacturing processes involving particular products and not to whole economic sectors. Moreover, these figures are based on MFN tariff averages and do not reflect preferential treatment. Since concessions under preferential agreements tend to focus on raw material inputs rather than on processed products, they may reinforce escalation effects. Changes in the tariff wedge, *i.e.* the absolute difference between the tariff at the higher and lower stages of processing, can predict the direction of changes in effective rates of protection.[24] Tariffication seems to have reduced tariff escalation across countries. Based on simple applied MFN averages, the wedge between raw materials and finished manufactured goods in developed countries declined after the Uruguay Round, especially in the European Union and United States. The European Union and Canada, though, exhibit increased wedges between semi-finished and finished manufactured goods, suggesting that reductions in tariff escalations for these countries only apply because of the tariffication requirement; and OECD (1995 and 1997*a*) find that tariff escalation still prevails in a number of agricultural product chains, such as coffee, cocoa and nuts, while they have been reduced in other cases. Overall these crude tariff indicators, especially in the case of the European Union,

Table 8. **Tariff escalation[1] in the Quad countries**

Per cent

	United States			European Union		
	1989	1993	1996	1988	1993	1996
Raw materials	3.2	3.3	6.2	6.0	6.0	10.9
Agriculture, forestry, fishing	3.8	4.1	8.3	8.5	8.3	11.9
Mining and quarrying	1.0	1.0	0.8	0.8	0.8	0.4
Manufacturing	2.3	2.3	3.2	5.2	5.4	11.7
Semi-finished	7.0	7.0	5.7	7.3	7.3	6.7
Finished	6.3	6.6	6.4	7.8	8.1	10.8
Total all products[2]	6.2	6.4	6.2	7.5	7.6	8.4
	Japan			Canada		
	1988	1993	1996	1988	1993	1996
Raw materials	3.8	3.8	3.9	3.4	3.3	6.8
Agriculture, forestry, fishing	5.1	5.1	5.0	3.6	3.5	5.6
Mining and quarrying	0.5	0.3	0.3	2.7	2.8	0.8
Manufacturing	3.4	3.4	3.5	2.5	2.4	5.7
Semi-finished	6.6	6.8	6.3	9.9	9.4	6.2
Finished	7.8	7.8	7.6	9.8	9.6	12.8
Total all products[2]	6.9	7.0	..	9.1	8.9	..

1. Based on simple applied MFN tariff averages.
2. The total for all products can differ from indicator 7 of table 6 (simple average applied tariff rate) for two reasons: *i)* they also include *ad valorem* equivalents (AVEs) for tariff quotas and variable charges; *ii)* there may be some missing values in the ISIC classification reporting. In the case of Europe, the fact that the production structure of Germany is used here constitutes a third potential source of difference.

Source: OECD.

have to be interpreted with caution. Nevertheless, they seem to indicate that the EU tariff schedule in the post Uruguay Round continues to exhibit peaks and tariff escalation (after having taken into account the tariffication requirement) and even show an increased level of distortion.

Greater transparency of non-tariff barriers

Non-tariff barrier measures (NTBs) have traditionally been more prevalent in the European Union and United States than in Japan and Canada. Outside the Quad countries non-tariff barriers are used to a lesser extent or even hardly used as in the case of New Zealand, Iceland and Turkey. Frequency and import coverage ratios[25] show a generalised decline in the pervasiveness of NTBs except for those countries that have recently joined the European Union. In the Community the textile sector remains the most protected by NTBs, while the pervasiveness of NTBs declined sharply in the processed food sector, reflecting tariffication.

One of the objectives of the Uruguay Round has been to ensure greater transparency and stricter discipline in the use of non-tariff barriers. A major achievement was the multilateral status given to the agreements on non-tariff measures,[26] ensuring a global coverage of the rules. To reduce uncertainty in the conduct of trade, including in the case of measures adopted by governments to counteract the effect of "unfair" trade practices, agreements on Subsidies and Countervailing Measures and on Anti-dumping were also concluded. Another major achievement of the Uruguay Round has been the prohibition of the use of Voluntary Export Restraints (VER) and comparable inter-industry arrangements.[27] A full assessment of all these agreements[28] and the implications for EU legislation and trade practice is not within the scope of this work. In the following, the focus is on trends in the use of different non-tariff barriers and on anti-dumping actions which are, in principle, instruments of trade defence.

Quantitative restrictions

While their importance had diminished considerably since the late 1980s, export restraints remained the predominant form of quantitative restrictions in 1996 in both the European Union and the United States (Table 9). Frequency ratios in both countries stood at around 11 per cent while, in Japan, non-automatic licensing remained the most important form of quantitative restriction. Apart from the remaining restrictions on agriculture and textiles and clothing, Community-wide quantitative restrictions remain only on a few categories of products from China and on imports of steel products from Russia, Ukraine and Kazakhstan, with which bilateral agreements exist.

Price control measures

With the progressive phasing out of VERs under WTO rules and the high degree of substitutability between Anti-Dumping or Countervailing Measures (AD/CVM) and VERs, the use of AD/CVM could become more frequent in the future. In addition, the process of tariffication of variable levies and quantitative restrictions applicable to agricultural products could increase resort to AD/CVM in this area. While the importance of AD/CVM and Voluntary Export Price Restraints (VEPRs) increased in the United States where such measures replaced the use of VERs, especially in the case of steel, the relative importance of these measures declined in the European Union. For the latter, both frequency and import coverage ratios of AD/CVM and VEPRs fell in the period from 1988 to 1996, from 2.6 to 0.9 per cent, and from 2.2 to 0.2 per cent, respectively. In the United States, though the frequency ratio fell over the same period, the import coverage ratio increased from 3.4 per cent in 1988 to 5 per cent in 1996. On the other hand, Japan hardly used AD/CVM or VEPRs between 1988 and 1996.

Table 9. **Pervasiveness of different types of NTBs in the Quad countries**[1]

Per cent

	Frequency ratio (F)[2]			Import coverage ratio (IC)[3]		
	1988	1993	1996	1988	1993	1996
United States						
All Non-Tariff Barriers (NTBs)	25.5	22.9	16.8	16.7	17.0	7.7
Core NTBs	25.5	22.9	16.7	16.6	17.0	7.7
Quantitative Restrictions (QRs)	20.4	18.1	10.9	13.7	10.2	2.7
Export restraints	19.5	13.1	10.8	12.9	10.1	2.7
Non-automatic licensing	0.0	0.0	0.0	0.0	0.0	0.0
Other QRs	6.6	5.6	0.6	1.1	0.2	0.0
Price Control Measures (PCMs)	17.8	10.8	7.6	3.6	7.3	5.2
Variable charge	0.1	0.0	0.1	0.1	0.0	0.1
AD/CVMs and VEPRs[4]	17.8	10.8	7.6	3.4	7.3	5.0
Other PCMs	0.0	0.0	0.1	0.0	0.0	0.1
European Union						
All NTBs	26.6	23.7	19.1	13.2	11.1	6.7
Core NTBs	25.2	21.8	15.1	10.9	9.0	4.2
Quantitative Restrictions	19.5	17.2	13.1	7.8	7.1	3.8
Export restraints	15.5	13.9	11.4	6.2	5.6	3.0
Non-automatic licensing	4.4	3.5	1.5	2.2	1.7	0.8
Other QRs	0.2	0.2	0.2	0.1	0.0	0.0
Price Control Measures	12.4	8.4	3.2	6.0	3.5	0.5
Variable charge	6.3	5.4	1.4	1.8	1.5	0.1
AD/CVMs and VEPRs[4]	2.6	1.9	0.9	2.2	1.3	0.2
Other PCMs	4.3	1.1	1.0	2.1	0.6	0.3
Japan						
All NTBs	13.1	12.2	10.7	8.6	8.1	7.4
Core NTBs	12.5	11.3	10.0	7.4	3.8	2.6
Quantitative Restrictions	11.7	10.5	9.2	6.6	3.0	1.8
Export restraints	0.3	0.1	0.0	0.2	0.0	0.0
Non-automatic licensing	8.9	8.9	8.6	1.3	1.3	1.3
Other QRs	2.8	1.6	0.6	5.4	1.7	0.6
Price Control Measures	0.8	0.9	0.7	0.7	0.8	0.8
Variable charge	0.8	0.9	0.6	0.7	0.8	0.7
AD/CVMs and VEPRs[4]	0.0	0.0	0.0	0.0	0.0	0.0
Other PCMs	0.0	0.0	0.0	0.0	0.0	0.0
Canada						
All NTBs	11.1	11.0	10.4	5.7	4.5	4.0
Core NTBs	8.9	8.2	7.2	4.1	2.5	1.9
Quantitative Restrictions	6.6	6.8	5.9	3.0	1.7	1.2
Export restraints	4.8	5.8	5.9	1.2	1.4	1.2
Non-automatic licensing	2.6	0.2	0.0	0.7	0.0	0.0
Other QRs	0.8	0.8	0.0	1.1	0.3	0.0
Price Control Measures	2.4	1.4	1.3	1.1	0.8	0.7
Variable charge	0.0	0.0	0.0	0.0	0.0	0.0
AD/CVMs and VEPRs[4]	2.4	1.4	1.3	1.1	0.8	0.7
Other PCMs	0.0	0.0	0.0	0.0	0.0	0.0

1. Indicators for 1996 are calculated after revising the 1993 Non Tariff Measures database by eliminating quantitative restrictions on "tariffied" products and updating the price control measures.
2. The frequency ratio (F) indicates the proportion (or percentage) of national tariff lines that are affected by a particular NTB or by a specified group of NTBs, irrespective of whether the products affected are actually imported.
3. The import coverage ratio (IC) indicates the share (or percentage) of a country's own imports that is subject to a particular NTB or any one of a specified group of NTBs.
4. Anti-dumping (AD) / Countervailing Measures (CVMs) and Voluntary Export Price Restraints (VEPRs).

Source: OECD.

The new anti-dumping regulation

The European Union has been a frequent user of anti-dumping measures under the GATT, and has used anti-dumping actions a lot more than either safeguards or countervailing duties.[29] However, while the number of outstanding anti-dumping actions has risen markedly in the United States since the early 1980s, it has remained relatively stable in the European Union (Figure 3). In mid-1999, some 180 measures were in force, which is considerably below the number of measures taken by the United States. The number of anti-dumping cases initiated by the European Union has shown a noticeable degree of counter-cyclical behaviour since the early 1980s (Figure 4). Resort to anti-dumping actions by the United States also appears to have been related to macroeconomic conditions. The correlation with macroeconomic developments is less tight, but still exists, for Canada and Australia.

In order to implement the 1994 Anti-Dumping Agreement of the GATT the EC Council adopted a new anti-dumping Regulation.[30] The Regulation entails some major changes with respect to the previous legislation in terms of fairer price comparisons to determine the dumping margin, stricter injury requirements, anti-circumvention measures[31] and a broader role for the "Community interest

Figure 4. **EU antidumping initiations and real GDP growth**[1]
1981-99, mid-year

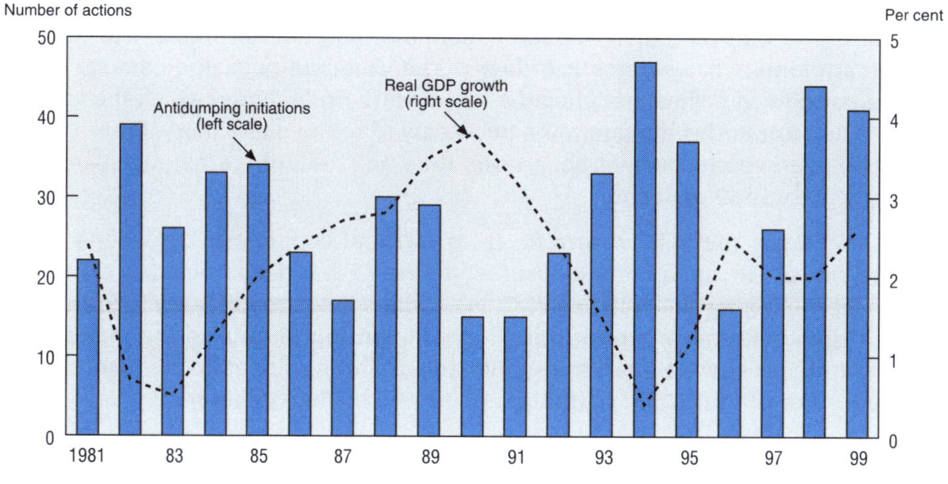

1. Antidumping initiations over 12 months to mid-year and one-year advanced real GDP growth.
Source: OECD.

test". Existence of injury does not give automatic entitlement to anti-dumping relief in the European Union. The Community will take anti-dumping measures only if these are considered to be in the Community interest. This degree of non-automaticity in the attribution of anti-dumping relief has traditionally distinguished EU from US anti-dumping law (Bronckers, 1995). Another issue not regulated under the WTO agreement but addressed by the EU legislation is that of actions against absorption of duties.[32] While EC rules are broadly in line with the WTO Agreement, significant differences remain in the areas of absorption of duties, circumvention of imposed measures, "Community interest" and de minimis import levels.[33]

Concerning the calculation of the dumping margin, the earlier EC legislation displayed two major biases when making comparisons between export prices and "normal values" (Bronckers, 1995). Firstly, price comparisons could be made at different levels of trade. For instance, "normal values" established at the level of sales to independent retailers could be compared with export prices established at the level of sales of independent distributors. Under the new regulation, the exporter can claim an adjustment whenever the different levels of trade are shown to affect price comparisons. The second bias originated from comparisons of weighted averages of the normal values prevailing during the period of investigation versus individual export transactions in the same period. This practice could give disproportionate weight to dumped exports. Under the new legislation comparisons are normally made between weighted averages.

Compared to WTO rules and US anti-dumping law, the injury requirement under EC law allows anti-dumping measures to be softened. Members may, under WTO rules, continue to impose anti-dumping duties corresponding to the entire amount of the dumping margin even if a smaller amount is sufficient to remove the threat of injury to a domestic industry. The Community is alone among major trading partners in having introduced a "lesser duty" rule, under which the level of the measure applied is the minimum necessary to remove the injury. From 1988 to 1992, the average measure imposed was thus only half of the average dumping margin which was 40 per cent.[34]

While in the WTO forum no international consensus could finally be reached on anti-circumvention measures, the new EC anti-dumping law continues to envisage applying such rules, a version of which had already been in force prior to the Uruguay Round negotiations. If circumvention of an existing measure is established, the new Regulation permits anti-dumping duties to be extended to imports of like products and parts thereof under certain conditions.[35]

Under the "Community interest" test, the overall interests of the Community are taken into account in deciding whether or not to apply anti-dumping measures, whereas there is no compulsory uniformity when applying a "public interest" test as set out in the WTO Agreement. Despite the existence of a "Community interest" clause, several authors have pointed out[36] that in a majority of cases the Commission seems to have equated the producers' interest with that of the Community. In early 1997, an upgrading process was initiated following growing criticism among market participants that EU anti-dumping procedures are rigid and one-sided. This new approach is based on a more rigorous economic analysis of products and markets and a consultation of interested parties, including importers, retailers, and users, while anti-dumping investigations have thus far relied primarily on information from the European producers which initiated complaints.

Rules of origin

While regional cumulation of origin already existed for EFTA/EU trade and trade between the Czech Republic, Hungary, Poland and the European Union recent changes have harmonised rules of origin among European countries. They have created a preferential territory for origin between the EEA (including the European Union), EFTA and CEEC countries, covering 28 countries. The reform consists in an alignment of the rules of origin in the different trade agreements and the linkage of all countries through diagonal cumulation. In contrast to bilateral cumulation, diagonal cumulation implies that producers can use imports from any country in the zone to produce an originating product. For instance, a producer in Hungary is now able to use Norwegian inputs to produce for export to a Community country. Efforts are currently underway to extend the new system to the countries covered by the Euro-Mediterranean agreements.

The changes are likely to further promote outward processing and assembly operations within this larger area and is another step in fostering integration within the European continent. The new system is probably most beneficial for the CEEC countries as it coincides with the abolition of EU duties on textiles and clothing and the dismantling of quantitative restrictions.

Agricultural protection remains high

Agriculture has traditionally been the most protected sector in the Community, even though the European Union is a major player in the world market. The 1992 reform of the Common Agricultural Policy (CAP) centred on reducing price support for cereals, oilseeds and protein crops, and beef, leading to a significant fall in the level of price support for grain by about one-third. In order to compensate for diminishing market price support, direct income compensation payments and set-aside measures were introduced. In conjunction with strong world market prices, the reform led to a steep decline in support to producers between 1995 and 1997. However, in the face of more adverse market conditions, support to producers has shot up again between 1997 and 1999.[37] Support also rose steeply in many other countries.

The Uruguay Round Agreement on Agriculture (URAA) has brought a number of changes to EU trade policy in this area. Under the Agreement, all border measures have to be converted to tariffs, while any further use of non-tariff measures is prohibited. Tariffs will be brought down by an unweighted average of 36 per cent, with a minimum reduction per tariff line of 15 per cent by the end of the implementation period (1 July 2000). Export subsidies and subsidised volumes, will have to be cut by 2001 by 36 and 21 per cent, respectively. Moreover, total trade distorting domestic support, aggregated across all commodities, will have to be reduced by 20 per cent in the six years following the agreement.

Despite the major achievements of the URAA, the immediate effect on agricultural trade is likely to be limited (OECD, 1995 and Hathaway and Ingco, 1995). There are several reasons for this:

- First, the base periods from which reductions in barriers to market access, domestic support and export subsidies were negotiated were periods of historically high levels of support and protection in most OECD countries. This was particularly the case for market access and domestic support where the base period is 1986-88, but it was also the case for subsidised exports where the base is 1986-90. High base levels translate into actual cuts, which are smaller than would be the case if more "representative" base levels had been used.
- Second, for important and therefore often politically sensitive products, countries applied the minimum cuts of 15 per cent.
- Third, although the tariffication of border measures together with the progressive binding of all tariffs will enhance transparency and predictability of the trading system, bound rates were often set well above the true tariff equivalent of the non-tariff measures that they replaced. This has allowed countries to vary applied tariff rates below the binding rate so as to stabilise the domestic market in much the same way as the European Union has done in the past with its system of variable import levies and export subsidies. Moreover, the URAA contains provisions, which allow for the imposition of additional tariffs should import prices decline or imports exceed base-year levels during the implementation period.
- Fourth, although the proliferation of tariff rate quotas (TRQs) increased access to some markets, TRQs have been under-utilised in most cases. In addition, they generate quota rents and introduce scope for discriminating between countries.
- Fifth, the discipline on domestic support was weaker than the other two pillars of the URAA because it was agreed only to reduce aggregate domestic support and not support for individual commodities, and some particular measures which are not trade neutral are exempted from the support reduction commitment.

Overall, the most significant move towards trade liberalisation should stem from the new disciplines concerning export subsidies. The European Union is the largest user of export subsidies and during 1997-99, it accounted for 90 per cent of the export subsidies notified to the WTO among the OECD countries that have export subsidy commitments, as compared to 1 per cent for the United States. The Union subsidises a wide range of agricultural commodities and processed products. Although the overall value of EU export subsidies were below permissible levels in 1995-97, the European Union overshot its entitlements for a number of products. While overall export subsidies for all commodities decreased substantially from € 8 billion in 1986-88 to € 4.8 billion in 1999, important export subsidies remain in the sectors that have been less affected by the CAP reform. In particular, export subsidies are estimated to have amounted to € 1.4 billion for sugar, € 1.3 billion for dairy products and € 0.8 billion for beef in 1999.

Implementation of the single market required substantial changes in the banana market since bananas were not subject to the CAP, nor to the common commercial policy. The Community's problem was to create a uniform system while keeping Member States' – notably France, Italy and the United Kingdom – special practices with respect to their favoured suppliers (the ACP countries). There was also a legal problem arising from mutually incompatible obligations from the Community's preferential (the Lomé Convention) and general (the GATT) arrangements, and the internal market rules. A two-tier import regime was adopted by the European Union, by which ACP suppliers no longer had an absolute advantage on some Member States' markets but still had a substantial tariff advantage on the Community's market over Latin American suppliers.[38] Moreover a system of import licenses was created and a 30 per cent quota was reserved for ACP suppliers. The new regime affected substantially the balance of interests and was opposed internally by Germany, and externally by Latin American exporters, which were backed by the United States. In 1996, the WTO upheld the EU's right to grant preferential tariff treatment to ACP countries, for which the European Union has a WTO waiver. However, most features of the EU's banana regime were found inconsistent with its WTO obligations, in particular the EU's complex licensing system for the distribution and ripening of bananas which discriminated against United States and Latin American companies. While the Union appealed against the WTO panel's findings and made further changes to the Common Market Organisation for bananas in 1998, the United States and Ecuador were granted authorisation for the suspension of concessions on EU trade in 1999. Recently, the European Union proposed further reform measures. A two-stage process is envisaged, including a TRQ to be replaced by a tariff-only regime by early 2006. Consultations among the interested parties are proceeding.

The agricultural policy agenda is moving forward both in the European Union and in the world community. New multilateral trade negotiations were launched in 2000 as a follow-up to the Uruguay Round and will aim at cuts in border protection and further reductions in export subsidies. In addition, a big challenge will come from eastward enlargement, which could lead to an expansion of the agricultural area by half and a doubling of the agricultural labour force. To address these issues as well as concerns about the preservation of the "European model" of agriculture, a new round of CAP reforms was launched as part of Agenda 2000 (see below). The Agenda 2000 reforms deepen and extend the 1992 CAP reforms by a further shift from traditional price-support measures to area and headage payments. Another aim is to develop a more comprehensive policy for rural areas. The reform allows for greater flexibility in the payment of EU subsidies to finance rural development and environmental measures. Better targeting will come at the expense of support to larger firms. It is uncertain, however, whether the reforms will be sufficiently deep to resolve the problem of exportable surpluses for some commodities.

Services are undergoing major liberalisation and e-commerce takes off

Liberalisation in the EU services sector is less advanced than in manufacturing. Core services' markets, such as telecommunications, air transport, and to a lesser extent financial services, have long been shielded from both internal and external competition. These sectors have recently undergone major liberalisation both inside the Community, with the Single Market Program in Services (SMPS), and outside, with the General Agreement on Trade in Services (GATS). The liberalisation approaches of the SMPS and the GATS differ significantly. The Treaty of Rome basically imposes the same rules for trade in goods and trade in services, and the SMPS requires liberalisation of cross-border and establishment-based trade in services within the framework of mutual recognition and minimal harmonisation. In contrast, the GATS defines four modes of supply (cross-border supply, consumption abroad, foreign commercial presence, movement of persons) and leaves open the possibility of liberalising only certain modes, thereby limiting the extent of liberalisation. Table 10 presents EU internal and external policies in the core service sectors. At the core of the GATS are specific commitments. Each member first negotiates which service sectors will be subject to the GATS market access and national treatment disciplines. It then negotiates what measures will be kept in place for sectors for which market access and/or national treatment is violated. Such limitations have to be specified by mode of supply. As there are four modes of supply, there are therefore eight opportunities for GATS Members to avoid full application of market access/national treatment. In addition to specific commitments, countries make "horizontal" commitments, *i.e.* they provide a list of laws and policies that restrict the use of a mode of supply by foreign suppliers, independent of the sector involved. Horizontal commitments often involve restrictions on the movement of persons (Hoekman, 1995).

Indicators of the extent of protection in the services sectors are difficult to obtain. The construction of frequency and coverage indicators has been constrained by the lack of suitably comprehensive inventories of trade impediments.

Table 10. **EU policies in core service sectors**

Sector	Internal market integration	Common external policy	Trade policy orientation	Multilateral commitments
Financial services	Yes, but not yet fully achieved in all areas and by all Member States.	Yes (authorisation and supervision of branches remain under national law).	Free access.	GATS.[1]
Telecom services	Yes, with differences due to monopolies in basic telecommunications.	Yes, though access conditions may vary because of national monopolies and tariffication practices.	Free access in liberalised areas.	GATS (value-added and other advanced services);[1] not for basic phone and fax services. Basic telecommunications agreement.
Air transport services	Yes, for EU nationals.	Rudimentary. Bilateral aviation agreements at national level.	Non-discrimination (slot allocation and aviation-related services) – reciprocity provisions.	GATS (auxiliary services);[1] traffic rights not covered by GATS.
Maritime transport	Yes, for EU nationals; temporary exemptions for island cabotage; several Member States tend to confine flag rights to their nationals.	Yes, but some Member States maintain cargo-shipping arrangements with third countries.	Free access, no cabotage rights – anti-dumping, countervailing and other trade remedy instruments.	Not yet.
Audio-visual services	Yes, for "European works".	Yes, with significant differences in Member States' interpretation and application of EU law.	Preferences for European productions – non-mandatory quotas.	No, MFN exemptions for "European works".

1. Subject to limitations on market access and national treatment.
Source: WTO and OECD.

However, some research has been carried out, based on the inventory of barriers provided by the GATS schedule of commitments. Several market access barriers are not captured in the schedules. Examples include labour legislation, tax regimes, restrictions on land ownership or use, licensing and related fees, existence and reach of competition policies, regulation of monopolies, etc. Moreover, the existence of bilateral sectoral agreements should be taken into consideration in assessing the overall degree of a country's openness. The following indicators are, therefore, fairly crude – even more so than the NTB indicators for trade in goods.

Hoekman (1995) used frequency and coverage ratios to give an indication of the degree of liberalisation implicit in the GATS.[39] The EU schedule seems to imply a lower degree of liberalisation as compared to the United States and Japan. Hoekman also calculated some very crude indicators of "tariff equivalents" by sector.[40] The sectoral figures show how cautiously these indicators have to be interpreted. The low "tariff equivalent" for the distribution sector in Japan shows that market access barriers and entry regulations, such as vertical restraints, are not well captured by the GATS schedules. Moreover, these figures are calculated solely on the basis of EU-wide commitments, while individual EU Member States may have attached additional restrictions to the schedule. The United States International Trade Commission (USITC) (1995) has compared the EU-wide commitments with the ones made individually by EU Member States. The results show a higher degree of "revealed relative restrictiveness" for the latter.

The Community has undertaken a series of sectoral studies to evaluate the impact of the single market on some core services. In the case of the air transport sector, the absence of a common policy has long delayed liberalisation and the third "liberalisation package" was only approved in mid-1992.[41] The EU study finds the results of the air transport liberalisation somehow disappointing, although the coincident timing of the liberalisation effort with adverse economic conditions has to be taken into account. Based on surveys and interviews, the most important remaining barrier is access to airport slots, which inhibits competition on existing routes as well as the development of new ones. In the past, also the granting of state aids was an important issue. Concerning openness to foreign competition, barriers at the EU-level are to some extent offset by more liberal provisions in bilateral air services agreements with individual Member States. The United States has signed or is currently negotiating open skies agreements with European States. The Commission, though, has received a mandate by the Council for a two-stage direct negotiation with the United States. The first stage envisages an agreement on a common regulatory framework for EU and US air carriers. A second stage, though only under explicit instructions of the Council, would involve negotiations on market access. Such negotiations have not yet started.

Telecommunication services have undergone significant liberalisation both at the EU-level, with the EU harmonisation starting in 1987, and at the multilateral level, with the GATS agreement covering advanced telecommunications services and the 1997 WTO Agreement on Basic Telecommunications. Under the WTO agreement, EU Member States have made a variety of individual commitments. Also financial market liberalisation has advanced. Following a decision by 52 governments accounting for 90 per cent of the global banking and insurance market, the Agreement on financial services concluded in December 1997 entered into force in March 1999. After the multilateral achievements in the basic and advanced telecommunications and financial sectors, a new push towards liberalising services will come with the new multilateral services round, which has started recently.

Electronic commerce develops at a rapid pace across OECD countries, although the most recent data show that, over the past years, the United States has been expanding its lead. For example the penetration rate of Internet hosts in the United States is now seven times that of the EU area and, as of March 2000, the United States had six times as many secure servers per capita than the European Union. The level and structure of Internet pricing, as well as infrastructure competition play a key role in stimulating demand for Internet products and services (Coppel, 2000). For instance, countries that are above the OECD average in Internet penetration are those characterised by unmetered local telecommunication charges. European countries not only charge metered local access prices, but also have higher consumption tax rates (close to 20 per cent in the European Union as compared to 10 per cent in the United States and 5 per cent in Japan; see OECD, 2000*a*).

The European Union has developed an integrated approach to promote the development of electronic commerce to reduce the lag *vis-à-vis* North America. Since issues of pricing of the "local loop" are important for the development of a critical mass of consumers, the European Union, at the Lisbon summit, set a concrete proposal to reduce the cost of using the Internet by the end of 2000. Moreover, the recently drafted Europe Action plan sets out a comprehensive strategy to address key barriers to the uptake of the Internet in Europe. The objectives, to be reached by 2002, include not only cheaper, faster and more secure Internet access, but also investment in skills for the information society, and the development of a critical mass of Internet users.

On the other hand, the diffusion of electronic commerce requires adaptation of national legal regimes and principles, or the development of new regulatory frameworks that are conducive to its diffusion. The European Union issued several directives in this area laying down standards for consumer protection and applying the internal market principle of free movement of services and home country control to electronic commerce. An example of the latter is the 1999 Directive on a Community framework for electronic signatures.[42] More recently, the so-called "E-commerce Directive" was adopted (the "Directive of the European Parliament and of the Council on certain legal aspects of Information Society Services, in particular electronic commerce, in the Internal Market"). The "E-commerce Directive" specifies harmonised rules to ensure that information society services benefit from the principles of free movement of services and freedom of establishment.[43] These rules include the definition of where operators are established, transparency obligations for operators, transparency requirements for commercial communications, conclusion and validity of electronic contracts and liability of Internet intermediaries.

The global nature of electronic commerce raises a number of new policy questions related to market access and the need for revising existing trading rules within the WTO framework (WTO, 2000*a*). Among the various issues treated in the WTO context, the European Union has expressed a clear position in support of a moratorium on new duties on the import of services provided by electronic means.[44] The European Union also supports the WTO position that the GATS principles apply to the order and delivery of services by electronic means, while goods ordered electronically and delivered physically, should fall within the scope of the GATT.

The transborder nature of electronic transactions inevitably brings out differences in EU regulatory approaches *vis-à-vis* third countries. This is evident in the area of protection of personal data. The 1998 Data Protection Directive allows national authorities in the European Union to suspend the transfer of data to third countries where the level of protection is considered inadequate. The contrast between the European and US regulatory approach that is based on industry self-regulation to protect privacy and the adaptation of unfair competition principles to protect database compilations has generated some tension and an intensive EU-US dialogue over the last two years. Only in March 2000 the European Union and the United States were able to reach a provisional agreement on the so-called "safe harbor" arrangement. Under the arrangement, the US Department of Commerce will establish a list of companies adhering to a set of data protection rules and related enforcement requirements, which the Commission has found to provide "adequate" protection. Adherents to the "safe harbor" will thus be secure against data blockages, EU businesses will know to which US companies they can transfer data without seeking other safeguards, while EU citizens will have the assurance that their data is being protected.[45]

Cross-border competition issues receive more attention

Trade liberalisation and the parallel globalisation of businesses have led to changes in the nature and workings of the trading system. There has been a significant increase in commercial practices with an international dimension such as mergers, strategic alliances and joint ventures. These can lead to an increase in anti-competitive practices across borders: cartels, abuse of dominant position, etc. The adoption of an international framework of competition rules would strengthen the multilateral trading system and promote more equal conditions of competition and market access. Even though the WTO has started to tackle these issues, progress in ensuring a global competitive playing field has been slow.

Nevertheless, some agreements contain competition-related rules. For example, the Agreement on trade-related aspects of intellectual property rights contains provisions on the control of anti-competitive practices or conditions in contractual licenses, relating to the transfer of technology or of other proprietary information. It also recognises the right of countries to regulate such practices through their domestic laws, and it provides for consultations and exchange of information between governments where there is reason to believe that licensing practices or conditions constitute an abuse and have an adverse effect on competition in the relevant market. The GATS contains provisions on consultation and exchange of information, similar to those in the TRIPs Agreements, and requires countries to ensure that monopoly services providers do not abuse their position in activities outside the scope of their monopoly privilege. A number of sector-specific trade agreements also include competition provisions. The scope of these provisions remains far too limited to provide for the effective control of anti-competitive practices at the international level.

Some countries have negotiated bilateral agreements on co-operation between their competition authorities. Such agreements have been negotiated in the Union both at the Community and the national level. At the Community level, for example, a co-operation agreement has been concluded with the United States. While the substance of these treaties has evolved, their scope remains also limited, as shown by recent competition policy-related trade conflicts between the European Union and United States. The EU's approach towards a further international strengthening of competition policy is described in Chapter IV.

Harmonisation of standards: a response to increasing technical barriers to trade

Technical barriers to trade (TBTs), *i.e.* trade barriers related to product standards and conformity, while falling in the EU due to the single market, have probably risen in relative importance at the global level in tandem with the liberalisation of border measures, demanding greater attention and action than in the past.[46]

With the Uruguay Round a new agreement on Technical Barriers to Trade was concluded, which was followed by a continuing rise in the number of notifications of mandatory standards and by an expanded coverage of conformity assessment procedures. Other major changes were the integration of the agreement into the overall WTO dispute settlement procedure, and the bringing in of standardising bodies, including private institutions, through the Code of Good Practice. Although not legally binding, the code assures greater visibility and transparency of non-regulatory barriers. Overall the new multilateral rules have strengthened the surveillance mechanism for standard-related measures, and have encouraged the use of internationally harmonised standards.

EU-wide co-ordination of national regulations was of particular importance to achieve the single market. The Community approach to removing barriers in the form of technical regulations rests on the principle of harmonisation of national rules. Mutual recognition agreements (MRAs) were developed to allow competent third country assessment bodies to take part in the EU's conformity assessment activities. MRAs are agreements on the mutual recognition of conformity assessment procedures for regulated products. The main features of the Community approach, together with some elements of the US federal system and the NAFTA, are presented in Box 2.

A study by Atkins (1996) assesses the incidence of TBTs for manufacturing and extractive industries sectors (3-digit NACE) through case studies and interviews. It shows that 79 per cent of intra-EU trade in non-agricultural products is potentially affected by regulatory barriers and, within this, 55 per cent of trade is also subject to non-regulatory barriers (Table 11). Case studies on the effectiveness of different approaches to removal of restrictions indicate that the mutual recognition principle seems to work only in the presence of Mutual Recognition Agreements (MRAs), or where mutually recognised standards have been developed.[47] Case studies of products under the New Approach Directives (see Box 2) show that this approach works well and has removed barriers, both regulatory and non-regulatory. Nevertheless, the study also reports some areas of concern related to the New Approach Directives. Complaints are mainly related to firms' difficulties to adapt, and lack of consistent enforcement and information.

Table 11. **Application of different approaches to removing technical barriers to trade**[1]

	Percentage share of intra-EU trade	Percentage share of EU manufacturing value added
Sectors with regulatory barriers		
Relying on mutual recognition of regulations	28	21
Harmonised by new approach	17	22
With detailed harmonisation (old approach)	33	33
Total	**79**	**75**
of which:		
Sectors also possessing non-regulatory barriers	55	44
Sectors with MRAs	10	7
Non-regulated sectors		
With non-regulatory barriers	2	1
With no apparent barriers	19	24
Total all products	**100**	**100**

1. A regulated sector is defined as a sector where a significant range of products are covered by technical regulations in at least one Member State, and which potentially creates barriers to trade.

Source: Atkins (1996).

Box 2. Different approaches to the removal of technical barriers to trade

The EU approach

The Community approach to removing barriers related to technical regulations rests on the principle of full harmonisation of national legislation, where uniform standards are set for all Member countries. There have been distinct approaches to harmonisation. The "old approach" incorporates all the technical details of the mandatory requirements in a directive. Under the "new approach" (introduced with the internal market), essential policy requirements for particular products are set out, while the development of detailed technical standards conforming to the requirements has been entrusted to standardising bodies.[1] Moreover, in 1989, the Community put in place the "global approach to testing and certification" which sets principles for conformity assessment. The global approach is based on international practice (ICO/IEC) and on mutually acceptable auditing procedures.[2] Goods manufactured pursuant to the requirements of the global approach are permitted to display a generic mark of conformity – the "CE" mark. All goods displaying that mark are entitled to circulate freely within Europe and are exempted from further conformity assessment by an importing nation.

The US Federal System

The US Constitution imposes a number of explicit restrictions on State commercial policies, such as the imposition of export or import duties without the consent of Congress (Sykes, 1995). The Congress is also empowered to regulate commerce with foreign nations and among States. State policies that are in contradiction with federal regulatory policy may be "pre-empted" by the Federal regime. The Congress has eliminated TBTs in many areas, *e.g.* drugs, television broadcast standards, design of tanker vessels, etc. Yet many technical barriers remain outside the scope of federal legislation, *e.g.* in the case of building codes, health regulations, pollution control regulations, etc. The absence of clear constitutional limitations on state powers in the regulatory arena has hampered the development of a coherent doctrine.

The NAFTA

The NAFTA agreement on technical barriers is broadly similar to the GATT/WTO provisions. NAFTA also contains separate agreements on Sanitary and Phytosanitary Measures and technical barriers, and applies the GATT principles. NAFTA goes somewhat beyond the GATT/WTO system, as parties are committed to harmonise their standards to the greatest extent possible, provided that this

Box 2. **Different approaches to the removal of technical barriers to trade** (*cont.*)

does not reduce "the level of safety or protection of human, animal or plant life or health, the environment or consumers" [NAFTA, TB Accord, Article 906(2)].

1. The European Standardisation bodies (CEN, CENELEC and ETSI) have the mandate to elaborate harmonised standards. These harmonised standards are not mandatory and are not necessarily based on international standards drawn up by ISO or IEC.
2. An interesting feature of the system concerns the procedure for opting out of a harmonisation or mutual recognition initiative. A nation seeking to do so must justify and present an explanation whether or not another party has complained. The procedural structure of escape clauses are analogous to the provisions in GATT that apply when a signatory deviates from international standards or enacts, in the absence of international standards, new standards that may significantly affect trade. They go beyond GATT obligations, however, by requiring a statement of justification. For a detailed discussion, see Sykes (1995).

As traditional means of protection are used to a lesser extent, it is important to understand whether policies like standard setting procedures can be and are used to protect home firms or markets.[48] If standards are adopted with no strategic purpose, regional and bilateral initiatives may, in the long run, facilitate negotiations over multilateral standards. In this context, the European Union offers one model and has made it an important element of its market access strategy. Chapter IV, on the future agenda, discusses recent EU initiatives.

The EU's market access strategy

In the mid-1990s, the European Union added flanking policies to the existing trade policy. The market access strategy provides for mechanisms and instruments to act more forcefully against trade barriers elsewhere. At the multilateral level, the European Union aims at strict compliance by its trading partners with WTO rules, at reductions of barriers to EU exports in the context of accessions of third countries to the WTO, and at shaping its strategy for the next round of multilateral negotiations, especially in the fields of agriculture and services.

Where this appears to be the most fruitful avenue to reduce barriers, the Union pursues bilateral negotiations. Mutual recognition agreements are, for instance, one way to reduce regulatory obstacles to trade. More broadly, the Community will continue to pursue agreements for improved market access or free trade agreements. A database has been created to compile information on existing obstacles to trade from various sources. Over 1 300 specific barriers have been identified so far and more than half subjected to a rigorous analysis.

In addition, the Commission issued a Trade Barriers Regulation, which allows firms to file complaints about trade barriers with the Commission. Where the Commission decides to open an investigation, it first tries to resolve the issue in an amicable way. Often the inclusion of a problem in the database is sufficient to initiate a dialogue with the country concerned leading to an acceptable compromise. Failing this, the complaint is brought before the WTO dispute settlement procedure. Until end-1999, twelve cases had been brought under the Trade Barriers Regulation. Market access is not only a concern for the European Union, but also for other countries. Box 3 provides some examples of recent trade frictions.

Box 3. The Community's involvement in trade frictions and conflicts

US-EU co-operation is developing through bilateral initiatives, such as the New Transatlantic Agenda, but major frictions still arise at the bilateral and multilateral level. While a few of these frictions receive large media coverage, most issues have been resolved bilaterally or multilaterally, without receiving attention. The United States and the European Union have, for instance, been by far the biggest users and beneficiaries of the WTO dispute settlement system. Between 1995 and mid-2000, 193 dispute settlement cases were initiated worldwide. Of these, the European Union has been actively involved in almost three-fifths of the total, as the complainant, the defendant or as a third party.

A significant number of the cases are between the European Union and the United States, partly reflecting the amount of bilateral trade flows. A longstanding cause for friction is the EU's Common Agricultural Policy. Two widely reported EU-US cases, concerning the imports of bananas (see above) and hormone-treated beef, raised sensitive issues such as EU preferences for developing countries and protection of EU consumers' health. Disagreement on whether bio-engineered foodstuffs should be banned concerns millions of dollars of trade. Even though the EU ban on the use of growth-promoting hormones in meat production is motivated by public health concerns, it has raised issues of backdoor agricultural protectionism. The ban was condemned by WTO rulings because the European Union failed to satisfy the new standard for trade restrictions based on health as formulated in the Safety and Phytosanitary Agreement.[1] While the European Union first flagged that it intended to comply with the ruling after a 15 month's implementation period, it offered compensation in May 1999 as it did not want to comply with the deadline until the completion of a new risk assessment. The trade sanctions are still in place. Recently, the European Union signalled that it is planning to take the dispute back to the WTO, claiming that it has now better scientific evidence concerning the health risks from eating hormone-treated beef.

Box 3. The Community's involvement in trade frictions and conflicts (*cont.*)

Trade tensions relating to food safety and other regulatory issues have become more frequent. Such disputes are harder to manage and settle, as they raise issues and concerns close to the heart of the public, such as cultural sensitivities or consumer fears. This experience prompted the United States and the European Union to establish an "early warning system" to minimise the impact of bilateral disputes and to head off future tensions. Similarly, concerning genetically-modified food, the European Union and the United States launched a joint exercise whereby approval procedures will be compared. In the future, products will be submitted for approval simultaneously on both sides of the Atlantic and regulators will consult throughout the process. In the multilateral context major frictions between the United States and the European Union have been related to the sanctions by the United States against Cuba and Iran/Libya. These frictions have been interpreted in the United States as EU moves to bring to the WTO dispute settlement cases, which are more political in nature than commercial.[2]

While many cases could be settled without creating any frictions, two competition policy cases led to considerable friction. These concerned the Boeing/McDonnell-Douglas merger and the proposed alliance between British Airways and American Airlines.

Implementation of the single market legislation had implications for external trade. This is the case, for instance, of the EU-wide harmonisation of standards. The introduction of the EU-wide ecolabelling programme led to complaints by foreign firms whose production processes differ from those used in European companies, while having comparable environmental impact.[3]

1. The WTO decision is based on the fact that the international scientific community has found no evidence of human health risk arising from the use of the five most common hormones.
2. See for example the opinion of Deputy US Trade Representative Jeffrey Lang (USTR document: iwp972465, 24 July 1997).
3. On 23 March 1992, the EU Council approved an EU-wide ecolabelling programme which permits a manufacturer to obtain an ecolabel for a product when its production and life-cycle meet general and specific criteria established for that particular product.

III. Economic effects of trade liberalisation

Economic integration has significant implications for the allocation of resources, patterns of specialisation and location of economic activities and, through all these channels, it affects growth. In this chapter, the focus is on the extent to which the process of internal and external integration can be associated with changes in trade patterns and how this may have affected overall economic performance.

Eyeballing trade indicators

Regional integration in Europe has had a strong impact on trade flows. The extent of regionalisation is commonly measured by the share of intra-area trade in total trade. Between the early 1960s and the late 1990s, the share of regional exports and imports in the respective EU totals rose considerably, from about 50 per cent to close to 65 per cent currently. Imports from the EFTA6 countries remained rather stable over this period, but those from other regions fell significantly. Trade shares with other industrial countries (excluding the EFTA countries) declined up to the mid-1970s and have since remained roughly unchanged, even though trade with eastern European countries was very dynamic in recent years (Table 12). Quite apart from the effects due to the reclassification of trade from inter to intra-area trade, accessions boosted intra-area trade over the medium term: for Greece, Portugal and Spain intra-area trade rose by more than 20 percentage points after accession, with similar developments after earlier accessions. Data spanning over a long period suggest that integration proceeded faster in recent years than over the 1970-85 period, but more slowly than in the early integration phase.

While the European Union is the largest trading bloc, its trade openness, once intra-area trade is subtracted, is not very different from that of the United States or Japan. Trade openness, as measured by the average shares of extra-EU nominal goods exports and imports in GDP, rose from 8 per cent in the early 1960s to about 10 per cent in the late 1990s (Figure 5). Currently, the NAFTA area and Japan show somewhat lower trade shares in GDP, with the former increasing its share over the period. Since the mid-1980s, the European Union and Japanese

Table 12. **The regional structure of EU trade**

Per cent of total

	EU12						EU15	
	1961	1970	1980	1990	1995	1998	1995	1998
	Exports							
Western Europe	56.5	65.2	66.5	70.3	66.0	65.4	66.1	65.5
EU12	43.3	53.5	55.6	60.1	56.8	56.4	. .	. .
EFTA6	13.2	11.7	10.9	10.2	9.3	9.0	. .	. .
Eastern and southern neighbours	13.8	10.9	11.4	7.5	9.0	10.6	9.2	10.9
Eastern and central Europe[1]	3.9	4.5	4.1	2.9	4.6	6.0	5.0	6.4
Mediterranean partners	5.5	3.2	3.9	3.0	3.3	3.5	3.2	3.4
ACP[2]	4.4	3.2	3.3	1.6	1.1	1.2	1.1	1.1
Rest of the world	29.8	23.9	22.1	22.2	24.9	23.9	24.7	23.6
Developing countries	16.5	11.2	13.8	11.4	14.7	12.1	14.4	11.9
Industrial countries	13.3	12.8	8.4	10.8	10.2	11.8	10.2	11.7
Total	100.0	100.0	100.0	100.0	100.0	100.0	100.0	100.0
	Imports							
Western Europe	49.7	59.0	57.2	66.4	64.9	63.3	65.9	64.1
EU12	40.2	50.4	49.2	57.1	55.9	54.6	. .	. .
EFTA6	9.5	8.6	8.0	9.3	9.1	8.7	. .	. .
Eastern and southern neighbours	11.8	9.3	9.9	7.4	8.3	8.5	8.2	8.6
Eastern and central Europe[1]	3.6	3.4	3.8	3.2	4.6	4.9	4.7	5.2
Mediterranean partners	3.7	2.2	2.6	2.4	2.4	2.4	2.2	2.3
ACP[2]	4.5	3.7	3.5	1.8	1.4	1.2	1.3	1.1
Rest of the world	38.5	31.8	32.9	26.2	26.8	28.2	25.9	27.4
Developing countries	19.4	15.2	19.9	13.0	13.7	14.1	13.1	13.6
Industrial countries	19.1	16.5	13.0	13.2	13.1	14.1	12.7	13.8
Total	100.0	100.0	100.0	100.0	100.0	100.0	100.0	100.0

1. Central and eastern European countries, Community of Independant States, Czech Republic, Bosnia and Herzegovina, Croatia, former Yugoslav Republic of Macedonia, former USSR and former Yugoslavia.
2. African, Caribbean and Pacific countries which have signed the Lomé convention.

Source: OECD, Foreign Trade Statistics database, June 2000.

trade shares have shown a decline. This is largely due to relative price changes of energy and raw materials. Including services, for which Eurostat estimates are available since 1985, raises openness to 12½ per cent, with transport and tourist exports and imports accounting for more than two-thirds of service trade flows. An indicator of exposure to foreign competition is provided by a measure which weights together export orientation and import penetration (Table A1 in Hoeller *et al.*, 1998). The exposure to foreign competition for the manufacturing sector was always higher in the European Union as compared to North America, even though North American trade exposure is catching up slowly to the European level. Japan

Figure 5. **Trade openness and specialisation**

Excluding intra-zone trade

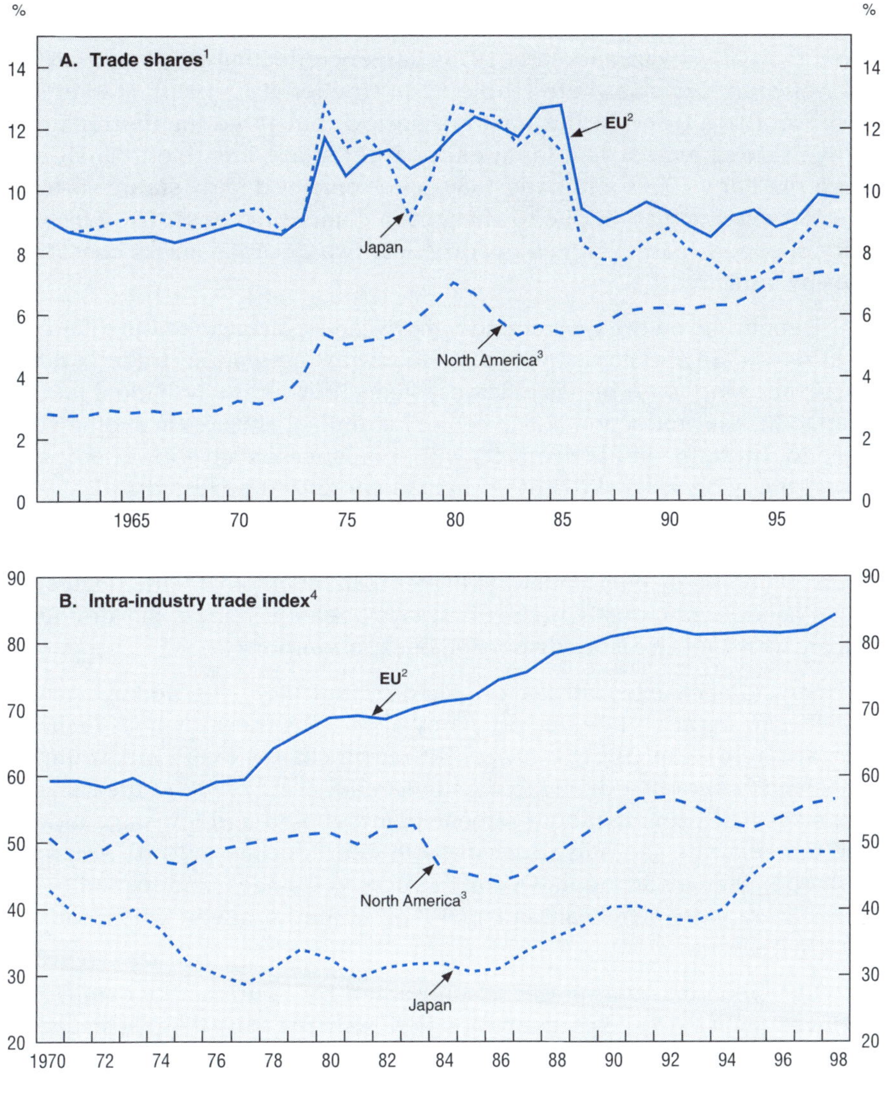

1. Average of goods export and import shares in GDP, current prices, per cent.
2. EU6 for 1961-72, EU9 for 1973-85, EU12 for 1986-94 and EU15 from 1995 onwards. EU includes ex-GDR from 1990.
3. Canada and the United States.
4. For total goods. The index varies between 0 and 100; it is high if a country's disaggregated exports and imports roughly balance.

Source: OECD.

continues to have a much lower exposure and, contrary to the European Union and the United States, its exposure has hardly changed since the early 1980s.

Both the European Union and North American manufacturing export market shares (excluding intra-zone trade) experienced a considerable decline between the early 1960s and early 1970s, largely reflecting very fast growth in a number of countries elsewhere (Table A2 in Hoeller *et al.*, 1998). Market shares have shown little trend in the ensuing period, but large fluctuations due to exchange rate changes. The Japanese market share has risen considerably between the early 1960s and early 1980s and remained fairly stable since then, again with large fluctuation due to changes in competitiveness. The EU's overall stability of export market shares over the last two decades masks considerable changes by industry.

Depending on the type of trade, there can be a considerable difference in terms of relocation and adjustment costs following integration. Trade in different products (inter-industry) brings efficiency gains, but within individual industries can lead to higher production in one country and plant closures in another. On the other hand, trade in similar products will in most cases have lower adjustment costs and the geographical distribution is likely to change less drastically. Measured by the Grubel-Lloyd index, extra-EU trade integration has led to a considerable expansion of intra-industry trade, with intra-industry trade within the European Union being only somewhat higher than for external trade (Figure 5). On the other hand, intra-industry trade has always been much lower in North America and Japan, with a much higher dispersion of export/import ratios.

Structural changes are also depicted by indicators of export specialisation (revealed comparative advantage). They show that the EU's high technology exports are below the OECD average, with little change over time, while North America largely kept its edge (Table A4 in Hoeller *et al.*, 1998). At the same time, Europe's specialisation in labour intensive, low-skilled and low-wage industries tended to rise, while showing a considerable trend decline in North America and even sharper changes in Japan. Overall, structural changes as depicted by these indicators were more significant in Japan than in the European Union, with North America in between.

European integration was accompanied by a substantial rise in foreign direct investment (FDI) flows, even though flows were considerably smaller than in North America until the mid-1980s. With the single market project the EU's FDI flows surged ahead and inflows and outflows surpassed North American flows by the early 1990s (Figure 6). However, much of these flows take place within Europe itself and excluding intra-EU flows, Europe's position as a host is well behind that of both North America and Asia. Furthermore, outflows are concentrated in the Union, European companies investing about twice as much within the European Union as they do outside (OECD, 1997*c*). The sectoral composition of the EU's FDI

Figure 6. **International direct investment flows**
Billion US$

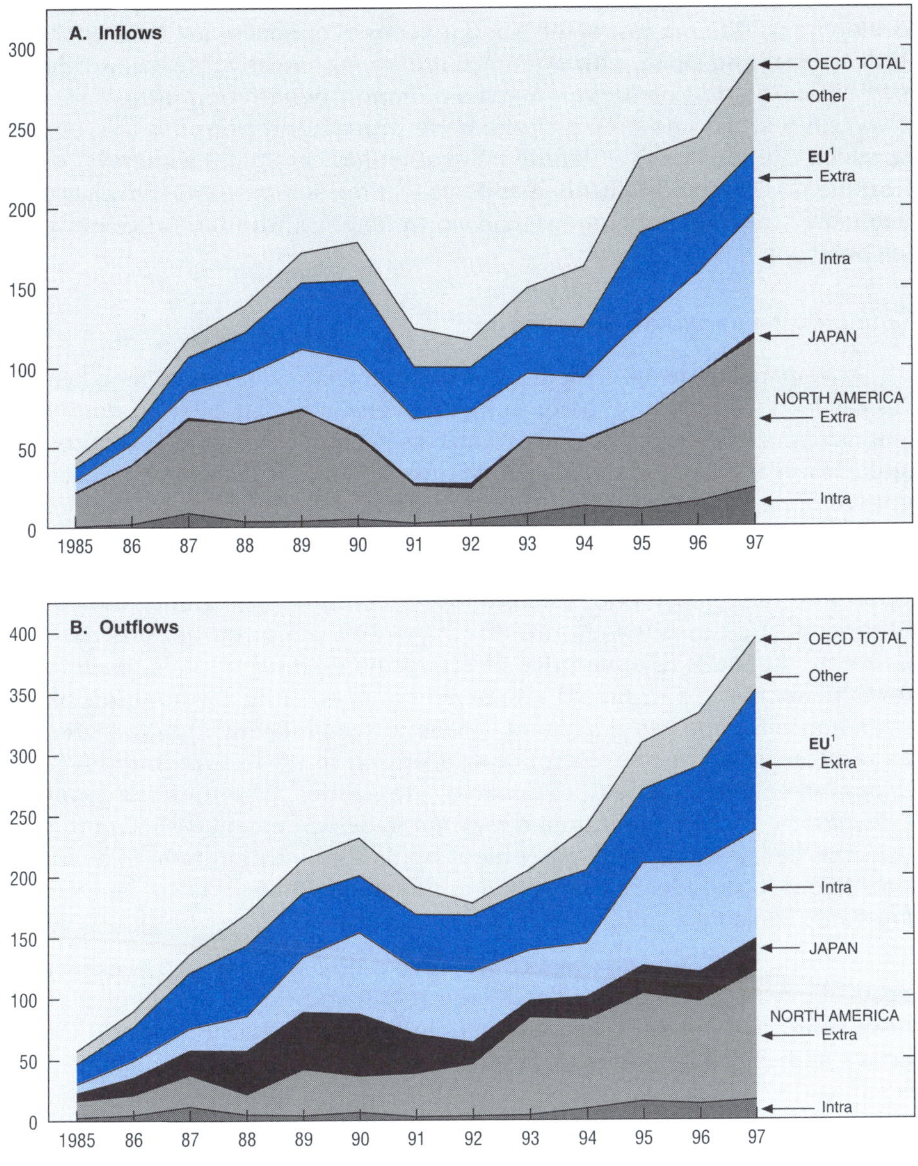

1. EU12 up to 1994, EU15 from 1995 onwards.
Source: OECD (1999), *International Direct Investment Statistics Yearbook* and OECD estimates.

flows is close to that of the United States and Japan. There is an increasing concentration of FDI in the service sectors, especially in finance, banking, insurance, telecommunications and business services.

Despite the rapid pace of regional integration, the EU's overall trade developments with the rest of the world in terms of openness are close to those in North America and Japan, with external trade having a relatively small weight in all three areas. In addition, developments of import penetration ratios (discussed below) suggest that the propensity to trade with other regions has also been rising, which implies that multilateral integration has continued alongside regional integration.[49] On the other hand, it appears that the Japanese economy has undergone more structural adjustment than North America, with the EU countries lagging behind in this respect.

Trade creation and trade diversion

Regional trade agreements, which discriminate in favour of member countries can lead to trade creation or to trade diversion of particular products. Trade creation refers to the substitution of a high cost supplier for a lower cost source of supply inside the integrated area. Trade diversion occurs if a higher cost source of supply from a partner country is substituted for a lower cost supply from third countries. Trade creation deepens the reliance on comparative advantage, while trade diversion does the opposite (WTO, 1995). The size of the diversion effects depends on the relative price changes following regional integration and the substitution elasticities between preferred and non-preferred imports. However, apart from the static relative price effects, regional integration is likely to raise growth performance and should also benefit third countries. In addition, regional integration in Europe has gone hand in hand with multilateral liberalisation, which has reduced margins of preference embedded in trade agreements. Finally, regional agreements can lead to positive externalities. Countries at a lower level of development can benefit from a regional trade agreement with a more developed one because the trade agreement binds a country's reform in an international treaty, it could lower opposition to reform and it could raise the credibility of reforms (Fernández and Portes, 1998 and Schiff and Winters, 1998).

Changes in demand shares have been used for a long time to examine the effects of integration [Jaquemin and Sapir (1988) and Neven and Roeller (1991)]. These shares can be split into domestic production (net of exports), intra-EU imports and extra-EU imports. A decrease in domestic production is indicative of trade creation, which may be due to an increase in intra-EU or extra-EU imports. On the other hand, a rising share of domestic production is characteristic of trade diversion, which may be either internal or external. Table 13 shows the evolution of consumption shares and internal and external import ratios for the manufacturing sector since 1970.[50] The latter are split into EFTA (including Turkey), non-

Table 13. **Import penetration ratios**

Average ratio of EU12 imports to total domestic demand for main industry groups

Industry	Period	Internal	External			Total
		EU12	Other European OECD countries[1]	Rest of OECD countries	Rest of world	World
Total Manufacturing	1970-77	12.0	1.9	2.7	2.8	19.4
	1980-87	16.2	2.7	3.8	3.8	26.4
	1990-97	20.1	3.3	4.7	5.7	33.7
Food, beverages and tobacco	1970-77	7.2	0.5	1.8	4.7	14.2
	1980-87	9.9	0.6	1.5	3.2	15.2
	1990-97	13.2	0.8	1.1	3.3	18.4
Textiles, apparel and leather	1970-77	12.6	1.3	1.1	5.3	20.4
	1980-87	18.4	2.4	1.4	9.7	31.8
	1990-97	22.2	3.6	1.4	18.8	46.0
Wood products and furniture	1970-77	5.8	4.3	1.4	3.8	15.4
	1980-87	8.1	4.4	1.6	4.5	18.6
	1990-97	9.5	4.4	1.6	5.9	21.3
Paper, paper products and printing	1970-77	5.9	6.4	2.9	0.4	15.5
	1980-87	8.6	6.4	2.6	0.9	18.6
	1990-97	10.2	6.4	2.3	1.3	20.1
Chemical products	1970-77	14.6	1.4	2.4	1.9	20.3
	1980-87	19.5	2.4	2.9	5.2	30.0
	1990-97	22.8	3.2	3.6	4.6	34.2
Non-metallic mineral products	1970-77	7.5	0.7	0.6	0.3	9.2
	1980-87	9.7	..	..	..	11.8
	1990-97	11.1	1.2	0.9	1.8	14.9
Basic metal industries	1970-77	11.7	2.1	2.6	4.1	20.6
	1980-87	16.9	3.7	2.2	4.4	27.2
	1990-97	20.2	4.7	1.8	6.3	32.9
Iron and steel	1970-77	11.1	1.6	1.3	1.2	15.2
	1980-87	16.3	3.0	0.7	1.8	21.7
	1990-97	20.7	4.2	0.7	3.5	29.1
Non-ferrous metals	1970-77	13.4	3.5	6.1	12.2	35.2
	1980-87	18.3	5.1	5.1	9.6	38.1
	1990-97	19.2	5.5	3.9	11.1	39.6
Fabricated metal products	1970-77	15.8	2.2	4.4	0.8	23.2
	1980-87	19.8	2.8	7.3	2.0	31.9
	1990-97	25.0	3.6	8.9	5.3	42.9
Metal products	1970-77	9.1	1.3	1.2	0.4	11.9
	1980-87	12.6	2.0	1.6	0.9	17.2
	1990-97	14.2	2.5	1.6	2.6	20.9
Professional goods	1970-77	26.6	7.3	14.6	1.8	50.2
	1980-87	34.4	9.3	26.7	5.1	75.7
	1990-97	39.4	10.9	27.9	9.2	87.3

1. Austria, Finland, Iceland, Norway, Sweden, Switzerland and Turkey.

Source: OECD, Foreign Trade Statistics database, June 2000; STAN database, June 1999 and OECD estimates.

European OECD and rest of the world import ratios. Overall, there was a continuing decline in the share of domestic production in apparent consumption, accompanied by an overall rise in intra as well as in external import penetration ratios, with about as much internal as external trade creation. Internal imports expanded about as fast as imports from the EFTA countries and non-European OECD countries, while trade creation was relatively faster for the rest of the world. As a comparison, in North America (the United States and Canada), internal trade advanced at about the same pace as in the European Union, but external trade advanced much faster for the rest of the world and the non-European OECD countries, while imports from EU countries lagged behind.

Intra-EU and external trade creation does not, however, permeate all sectors and regions. This is, for instance, the case for the food, drink and tobacco category, where internal import penetration rose considerably, while falling somewhat for the non-European OECD countries, declining considerably for the rest of the world and rising somewhat for the EFTA countries. The same occurred also in North America, even though to a lesser degree (Table A5 in Hoeller *et al.*, 1998). On the other hand, external import penetration rose significantly in the textile, footwear and leather sector, despite the high level of protection. Another sector where internal import penetration rose considerably, while external imports declined in relative terms, is non-ferrous metals. Overall, extra-regional trade expanded rapidly, but to a lesser extent than intra-regional trade, and any bias against extra-EU imports due to regional integration was probably minor. This was to be expected since external protection in manufactured goods was already fairly low in the early seventies and internal liberalisation of the manufacturing sector had already gone a long way.

Gravity models, which model trade as a function of geographic distance, income and population have also been used to assess the trade creating and diverting effects of regional trade agreements, typically by adding dummy variables for membership in such agreements. Bayoumi and Eichengreen (1995),[51] for instance, find that some trade diversion occurred between the initial period of the EEC and the late 1960s, but not thereafter. Later on, accessions by the United Kingdom, Ireland, Denmark and Greece led to some trade diversion, but no evidence of trade diversion was found after Spain and Portugal joined.

What could be more worrying in this context are trade developments between eastern European countries and the European Union in recent years. The lifting of the iron curtain and liberalisation in these countries led to a strong reorientation in trade flows. The share of trade among the eastern European countries collapsed until 1994 and recovered afterwards, while that with the European Union soared, both for exports and for imports (Figure 7). These two changes were accompanied by an equally important collapse in trade with MFN countries. While a sharp fall in trade with the former Soviet Union countries was to be expected,

Figure 7. **Trade of eastern Europe**[1]

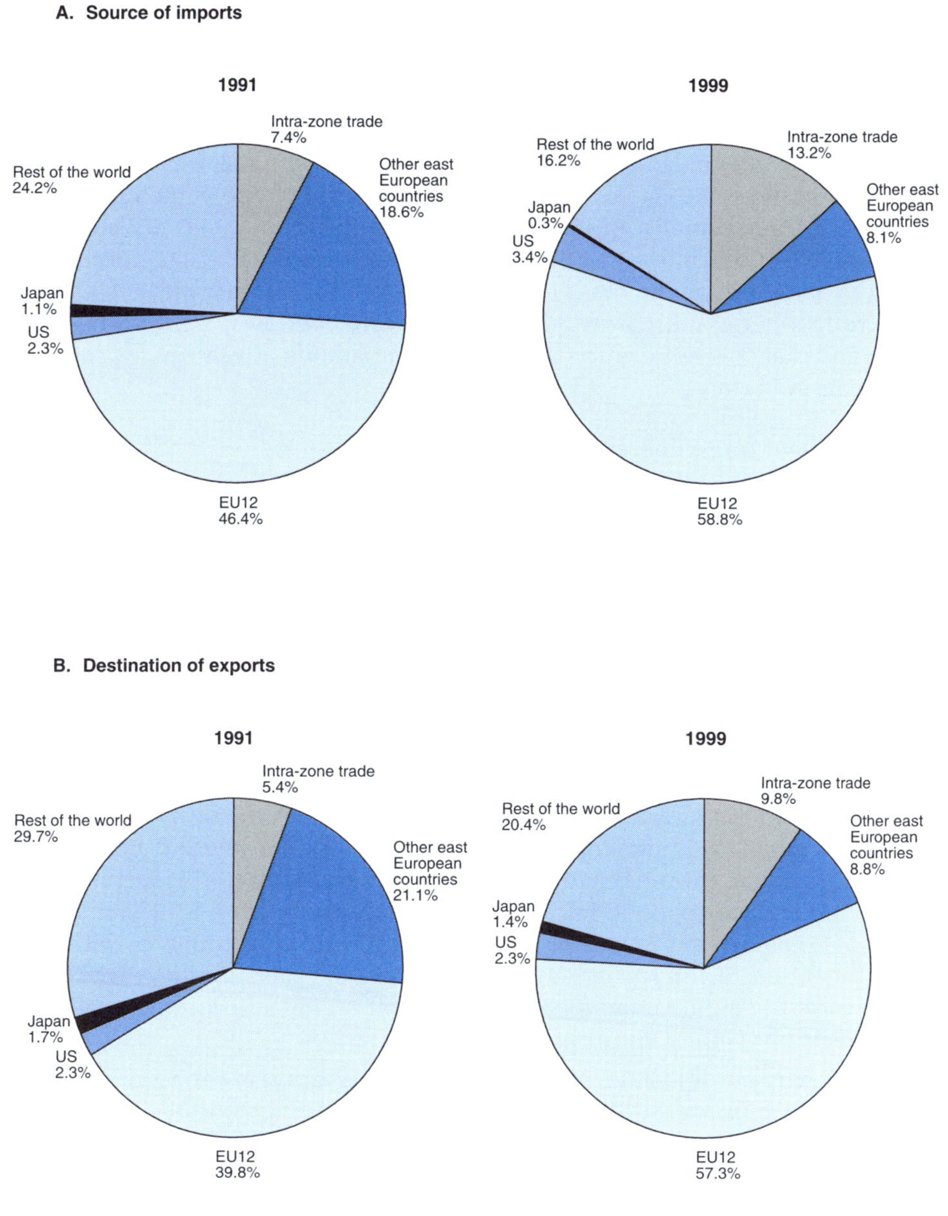

1. Czech and Slovak Republics, Hungary, Poland and Romania.
Source: IMF, Direction of Trade Statistics, May 2000.

trade developments with the largest and/or most dynamic economies in the world (United States, Japan and Pacific Asia) were subdued. With the economic recovery of the eastern European countries, fairly rapid output growth could have ensured that trade with the rest of the world would also grow substantially, despite the preferential agreement with the European Union. In the absence of data on apparent consumption, trade intensity and propensity indices can shed light on this question. The trade intensity index measures whether a country's trade with a certain region is higher or lower than its importance in world trade, while the propensity to export index measures to what extent there is still a rise in their propensity to export extra-regionally. Based on the developments of these two measures, Messerlin (1996) concludes that there is a risk that trade diversion has occurred. It should be stressed, on the other hand, that these trade developments could also partly reflect geographic proximity, with trade further away developing more slowly, and that it is not easy to determine comparative advantage for countries undergoing swift transition.

Investment and trade liberalisation

Numerous links exist between trade and foreign direct investment (FDI), even though FDI is by and large not "trade by other means". The links between trade and FDI are reviewed in Box 4. Empirical work on the effects of European integration on FDI has mainly dealt with the impact on inter-regional FDI.[52] Earlier research points to increased inward FDI flows from the United States following the formation of the European Community, while studies at later stages in the European integration find more mixed results. Studies of the impact on intra-regional FDI are rarer and constrained by data shortages. Again the results are mixed and depend on the period considered. Some studies focus on changes in the number of foreign subsidiaries of EU firms established in other EU countries in the pre-1985 period and point to some "investment diversion". On the other hand, a study by Agarwal *et al.* (1995) shows that in the post-1985 period there is no evidence that the growth of extra-EU FDI into the European Union in the sectors where intra-EU trade has expanded has been at the expense of extra-EU FDI into other developed countries.[53] Studies of outcomes for individual countries within the region have been given less attention. The results are mixed, with Ireland, Spain and Portugal benefiting from large intra and inter-regional flows, while no investment effects were found for Greece.

Gravity models have also been used to assess the impact of European integration on bilateral FDI flows. CEPS (1996) models the geographical distribution of outward FDI and exports for France, Germany, Japan, Sweden, the United Kingdom and the United States. The importance of the European Union destination market for the European countries in the sample is considerable. FDI outflows from France to the European Union appear to be six times higher than would be expected on the basis of income, population and distance alone. The effect is

Box 4. Trade and foreign investment

FDI is in many cases a complement to trade, including, for instance, local offices or distribution channels. Traditional FDI theory also motivates the decision of a firm to engage in FDI abroad on the basis of some cost advantage that the multinational enterprise (MNE) might have in the foreign market. Cost advantages can be due to ownership specific advantages, internalisation advantages and locational advantages.[1] Regional integration affects locational advantages directly and ownership advantages indirectly, the latter by strengthening the competitiveness of firms. Recent models of multinationals and two-way investment between countries have emphasised the role of the interaction between economies of scale and trade costs on MNEs' activity. The higher firm-level fixed and trade costs relative to plant-level economies of scale, the higher will be the level of FDI. According to these models, increased convergence in size and endowments led by integration intensifies MNEs' activity, especially in those sectors with high firm-level fixed costs. On the other hand, the lowering of trade costs will tend to increase trade relative to FDI, especially in those sectors characterised by large, unexploited economies of scale.[2] Hence, the net effect of regional integration on intra-regional FDI flows is ambiguous and will vary by sector.

To the extent that regional trade agreements also entail capital flow liberalisation, intra-regional FDI will be encouraged. Liberalisation measures include the direct elimination of restrictions on inward FDI, the introduction of national treatment provisions, the elimination of trade-related investment measures and the establishment of a common strong framework of investor rights. On the other hand, inter-regional FDI flows would be expected to increase if the overall level of average protection increases after integration, or if integration raises fears about future levels of protection (*e.g.* in the debate on "Fortress Europe"). Moreover, a large "internal" market, by fostering demand (a larger number of consumers) and supply linkages (lower average costs), reinforces the locational advantage of the integrated area.[3] In addition, inward FDI might rise due to strategic considerations. If regional trade integration causes trade diversion, outside firms losing export shares to region-based suppliers might respond with investment creation.

Dynamic growth effects of economic integration could raise the overall impact of regional integration on FDI flows. On the one hand, capital-induced growth effects are reinforced by capital inflows and spillovers, while, on the other hand, growth in the region makes it an even more attractive location, thereby stimulating both intra-regional FDI flows as well as inward flows from the rest of the world.

1. Ownership advantages are linked to the product or process characteristics or to intangible reasons such as brand name and quality. Internalisation advantages are driven by the exploitation of intangible assets such as knowledge of local markets, consumer preferences and business practices. Locational advantages relate to trade barriers, cheap factors of production and ease of access to consumers.
2. This is an effect equivalent to the one taking place in the presence of tariff-jumping FDI as referred to in traditional FDI theory. Intra-regional investment flows motivated by tariff-jumping are expected to contract since the liberalised trade within the region makes them relatively less attractive than direct trade.
3. As suggested by the new economic geography literature, the relocation of economic activities following integration will depend on the net effect of centripetal and centrifugal forces. To the extent that a pattern of a centre (where production activities are located) and a periphery emerges, differences in locational advantages might be reinforced by inward FDI flows in those areas. In this case, some member countries could experience investment diversion.

eight times higher for the United Kingdom and two times for Germany. Dividing the sample into pre and post-single market periods, results indicate that during the single market programme, in the year of its peak effect, FDI to the European Union increased by 100 per cent for France, 80 per cent for Germany, and 200 per cent for the United Kingdom.

In conclusion, the impact of trade integration on FDI is multidimensional, and from the empirical evidence only a few patterns emerge clearly. Even if trade and FDI can be alternative ways of supplying a foreign market, the empirical evidence points to a relation of complementarity rather than substitutability between the two; FDI has increased strongly, but this is due to the market size and growth effects of integration rather than to fears of a "Fortress Europe"; and there is no strong evidence that the increased intra-EU FDI has diverted investment flows away from one or more destinations outside the regional integration agreement. Finally, FDI is largely not "trade by other means" or a redistribution of production from one location to another. Most direct investment involves mergers and acquisitions in Europe and elsewhere. While market access is always part of the motive of mergers and acquisitions, it is also an industrial strategy to increase the size of a firm. In this way, cross-border acquisitions have more in common with domestic mergers and acquisitions than they do with traditional FDI. This raises many issues which go considerably beyond the trade-related issues raised above. Differences in capital market structures are still large across Europe as are corporate governance rules and their institutional setting. While on the agenda, a common European-wide framework concerning company law has yet to be established and investment funds are still restricted in their investment decisions even in the single currency area. Also privatisation of state-owned enterprises is far from complete in many EU countries. The influence of these factors is likely to be as important or even more important than trade liberalisation in shaping FDI flows.

Trade and growth

The surging exchange of goods, services, capital and ideas has fostered strong interdependence among countries and trade is likely to be an important determinant of long-term growth performance. While international trade liberalisation progressed little over the last decade, though it received a boost recently with the conclusion of the Uruguay Round, interest in the nexus between trade and growth has been renewed by regional integration schemes, such as the EU's internal market programme or the North American Free Trade Agreement. Research on potential gains from such regional integration schemes has shown that they should be considerable. On the other hand, while the large amount of empirical work on trade and growth has found so far only a few robust trade effects, recent work seems to be more promising. A review of this empirical research is provided in Box 5.

Box 5. Trade and growth: is there a link?

Trade liberalisation can affect growth if it alters the return to capital accumulation. In a neo-classical growth framework this leads to medium-term investment and growth effects. Trade liberalisation will induce a more efficient allocation of resources and this in turn will have a one-shot positive impact on the level of per capita income, thereby stimulating saving and investment. In a framework with endogenous capital accumulation economic integration may have, instead, long-run growth effects. Any policy which affects the costs and benefits of capital formation can have a long lasting impact and, if the term capital is used in its broader definition, economic integration can affect growth rates through three different channels: physical capital formation (integration-induced investment-led growth), human capital formation (integration-induced skills-led growth) and knowledge capital formation (integration-induced technology-led growth).

While it is only recently that tools have been developed to evaluate the link between long-run growth and trade, empirical work on the effect of trade liberalisation on economic growth has a long tradition. The large number of case studies reviewed by Edwards (1989) document the experience of many countries which have undergone trade liberalisation efforts, and provide a fairly impressive amount of qualitative evidence pointing to a positive relation between trade liberalisation and growth.

The vast quantitative empirical literature of the 1970s mainly used cross-country regressions to look at the link between openness and growth. This literature has failed to provide a convincing theoretical framework to address the link between trade and growth and it mainly relied on simple correlations between exports and GDP growth, or on correlations between a set of proxies for openness or trade policy indicators and long run growth. Studies looking at correlations between export shares or export growth and GDP growth (surveyed by Edwards, 1993) usually find a strong link between openness and growth. However, the lack of a theoretical framework, and issues of causality and of spurious correlation, have undermined the credibility of the results of this work. Another line of research has linked measures of trade policy with growth and has generally been carried out in the context of the so-called regressions *à la Barro* (Barro, 1991). This framework allows the estimation of the cross-country speed of convergence of per capita income levels. After having controlled for country differences in initial conditions, such as the level of human capital, other variables are added to see if they affect long run growth. Levine and Renelt (1991) thoroughly examined the methodological, conceptual and statistical short-comings of cross-country regressions, and concluded that they should be viewed as suggestive of empirical regularities and not as describing behavioural relationships. The same authors (1992) criticise the *ad hoc* framework used in these cross-country regressions and show the lack of robustness of most of the correlations found in this literature. They find that openness proxies (export, import and total trade to GDP shares), as well as some trade policy indicators, are robustly correlated with the investment share, but do not have an independent relation with GDP growth. They suggest that if a robust link between trade and growth exists, this is based on the correlation between openness and physical capital accumulation as proxied by investment shares.

Box 5. Trade and growth: is there a link? (*cont.*)

The new trade and endogenous growth literature focuses on the channels through which trade liberalisation and economic integration can affect growth. Empirical studies have basically been carried out within the framework of growth accounting equations (Baldwin and Seghezza, 1996*a*) and have relied on either cross-section or time series data, and a few recent attempts combine the two dimensions. If the impact of trade and trade policy on growth is indirect, the proper way to assess it would be to estimate a full system of simultaneous equations in which trade affects the accumulation of capital in a broad sense. A full equation system has never been estimated but Baldwin and Seghezza (1996*b*) use three stages least squares regressions to endogenise physical capital and control for technological progress. This and other studies (*e.g.* Lee, 1993 and 1994) conclude that, using cross-country data, one can find positive evidence of integration-induced investment-led growth but not an independent effect of trade barriers on technological progress.

Time series and pooled regressions have been estimated both in growth rates and in levels using co-integration techniques. This work tests directly for the link between trade and growth through the technology channel, and points to some direct positive impact of openness on innovation. Coe and Moghadam (1993) conclude that trade and capital broadly defined account for almost all the growth in the French economy in the last two decades; and Coe and Helpman (1995) find that international knowledge spillovers, defined as trade weighted averages of foreign research and development (R&D) capital stock, affect growth in a panel of developed countries. Although the use of co-integration techniques in these studies allows a direct test for a long-run relationship between trade and growth, one needs to be very cautious in interpreting this kind of evidence. On the one hand the mismeasurement of the explanatory variables, especially the R&D stock, can be correlated with the proxies used for openness, thereby generating spurious correlations; on the other hand, co-integration techniques applied to pooled regressions are not yet well developed. Other work by Edwards (1998) seems to be more promising. The author, using a large panel of countries, finds a correlation between nine alternative openness and trade policy indicators and productivity growth which appears to be robust to differences in samples, estimation technique, time period and functional form. However, the results related to causality have remained somewhat open and Rodríguez and Rodrik (1999) have questioned the robustness of the indicators used. Frankel and Romer (1999) have addressed the endogeneity problem by focusing on geographic factors that could determine trade. Geographic factors, such as proximity to a large market, are unrelated to trade policy and trade policy is unlikely to be related to geography. Geographic characteristics are thus ideal to obtain instrumental variable estimates of the trade impact on growth. Their results suggest that trade has a large, though only moderately significant impact on growth.

Box 5. **Trade and growth: is there a link?** *(cont.)*

The empirical literature on trade and growth suggests that, while the intuition of a positive link between trade and growth is justified, this link is indirect. It is crucial to assess through which channels trade operates to be able to infer policy conclusions. For the moment empirical work points to a robust relation between openness and capital accumulation. Work on the impact of openness on total factor productivity growth, has shown that, even if positive, such an impact seems to be relatively less important than other factors, such as human capital formation and catching-up (Ahn and Hemmings, 2000).

While the early analysis of economic integration focused on the gains from increased specialisation according to comparative advantage and lower trading costs,[54] recent advances in trade and growth theory have stressed the importance of imperfect competition, economies of scale, product diversity and dissemination of technical progress. In the presence of economies of scale, an increase in market size will allow production at lower average costs. The Commission's assessment of achieving the single market in the late 1980s, for instance, concluded that about a third of industry could benefit from scale economies, yielding aggregate savings of 2 per cent of GDP (European Commission, 1988). Large gains from scale economies were also thought to boost growth in Canada after conclusion of the US-Canada Free Trade Agreement. Trading costs have been lowered further in the European Union with the introduction of a single currency.

Removing trade barriers is also likely to induce increased competition, causing prices to converge towards levels more consistent with economic and technical efficiency. Before the Single Market Programme many service industries in the European Union, as well as most public procurement markets, were shielded from foreign competition. Evidence of a lack of deep integration in the European Union is given by the large dispersion of prices across EU member countries.[55]

Larger markets are also likely to induce increased variety and specialisation in producing inputs (Romer, 1987). Apart from the welfare effects stemming from the availability of new product varieties, the new trade and growth literature predicts a link between the nature of trade and growth. A rise in intra-industry trade in intermediate inputs raises efficiency in production. If this increased specialisation takes place in the research sector, this will boost innovation activity. Backus *et al.* (1992) show a positive correlation between productivity growth and intra-industry trade over a cross-country sample after having controlled for scale effects. This channel could be of particular relevance for Europe where intra-industry trade, especially at the intra-European level, is high. In addition, trade may help in the process of technological dissemination and raise incentives for industrial research.

There is a general belief that European integration has promoted growth. Evidence in terms of productivity and investment trends, as well as empirical studies of growth and convergence in the European Community, point in this direction.[56] A few studies have tried to test the growth effects of European integration. In Coe and Moghadam (1993) the trade proxy is intra-European trade as a share of European GDP. This variable is thought to capture the beneficial effects from enhanced competition and economies of scale.[57] Baldwin and Seghezza (1996*a*) test for a differential impact of knowledge spillovers on the growth of countries belonging to the European regional area. Building on the analysis of Coe and Helpman (1995), they add a multiplicative European dummy to the stock of foreign R&D. Their results do not allow a formal assessment of the impact of European integration and their positive point estimates of the European dummies might capture many effects other than European integration. Similarly, Henrekson *et al.* (1997) find a positive growth effect for countries forming part of the European Union, but the effect is not always robust and depends on the specification of the empirical model, while Vamvadakis (1998) finds no effect at all. On the other hand, Italianer (1994), by adding to physical capital accumulation and labour input a proxy for trade integration and a general openness variable, finds a strong and positive impact of both the openness and integration proxies.[58] The results, though, could reflect the correlation of the openness variables with both human capital and technological progress, and may thus not play an independent role.

In the exercise detailed in Annex II, further evidence on the link between trade indicators and overall growth in the context of an aggregate production function approach is provided. A cross-country panel of eleven EU countries is used in estimating a production function in growth rates over the period 1970-95. Following Italianer (1994), a proxy for openness (O, defined as the share of total trade in GDP) and a proxy for European integration (I, defined as the share of area trade in total trade, corrected for successive enlargements) is added to the regression. In addition, an intra-industry trade index (S) is included in the production function estimate. Hence, an attempt is made to control some of the channels through which trade could have an indirect impact on growth (physical capital formation, investment in research and development, country-specific differences in technical progress) and test whether additional gains to the eleven European countries could stem from increased trade on a multilateral or on a regional basis.

The estimates show that the openness variable has a significant and positive coefficient which is robust to changes in sample period and estimation methods. The intra-industry trade index is also positive over the whole period but the coefficient decreases dramatically when the integration variable is introduced. This is understandable, given that intra-Community trade is to a large extent intra-industry trade. On the other hand, the integration variable is positive but never significant. Hence, there is no evidence of an additional independent impact of regional trade integration apart from that stemming generally from the exploitation of scale economies. By breaking down the sample period it appears that scale economies have played a role only in the 1970s, while investment in R&D starts playing a role only later (see equations 1 and 2 in Table 14).

In conclusion, there is evidence that openness in general, rather than regional trade integration, has favoured aggregate growth in Europe. A 1 per cent change in the openness variable would imply on average, across time and across countries, a 0.09 per cent increase in GDP growth, compared to a 0.44 and 0.42 per cent elasticity estimates of employment and the physical capital stock respectively. The openness coefficient tends to vary across countries, being higher for the EU6 and Portugal. The magnitude of the estimated coefficients have to be taken cautiously, given the great heterogeneity across countries and the heroic assumption of a common European production function. Finally, given that the R&D variable only becomes significant in the 1983-95 sample, greater attention should now be given to the R&D growth channel and to the role that trade might play in the diffusion of technology.

Table 14. **Trade and growth in a panel of eleven European countries**[1]

Fixed effects estimator with different time slopes for the R and S variables

$$\Delta \ln Y = \alpha_0 + \alpha_1 \Delta \ln E + \alpha_2 \Delta \ln K + \alpha_3 \Delta O + \alpha_4 \Delta S + \alpha_5 \Delta I + \alpha_6 \Delta \ln R$$

	α_1	α_2	α_3	α_4	α_5	α_6	Rbar**2	DoF
(1)	0.38	0.42	0.09	0.13	0.02	0.01	0.35	230
	(6.45)	(4.96)	(3.48)	(2.05)	(1.38)	(1.12)		
				1970-82		**1970-95**		
(2)[2]	0.38	0.43	0.09	0.22	0.02	0.00	0.36	228
	(6.41)	(5.09)	(3.61)	(2.92)	(1.58)	(0.00)		
				1983-95		**1983-95**		
				0.00		0.05		
				(0.00)		(2.15)		

1. **Variables:** Y = real GDP; E = total employment; K = private sector capital stock; R = private sector expenditure on research and development; O = share of total trade (imports + exports) in GDP; S = intra industry trade index; I = share of area trade in total trade which takes into account successive enlargements.
Sample: Yearly data (1970-95) for eleven EU countries (Luxembourg excluded). T-statistics in parenthesis.
2. In equation (2), the coefficients of the specialisation index and of the R&D variable vary between the two sub-periods, while the other coefficients are estimated over the whole sample period.

Source: OECD.

Trade and employment

Increasing wage inequalities in the United States and rising unemployment of unskilled labour in Europe have generated a lively debate on the impact of trade with low wage countries. These labour market trends could also be due to the adoption of new technologies (*e.g.* information technologies) which can be skill biased. The relative contribution of these different explanations is a question of empirical assessment, even though they may not be independent forces (Burda and Dluhosch, 1999). International competition, for instance, could induce firms to innovate.

Theory suggests strong trade and wage linkages, which can occur through different channels: changes in relative output prices affecting relative factor prices (relative wage of skilled and unskilled labour) as generally analysed in the Heckscher-Ohlin-Samuelson framework;[59] "outsourcing" and "delocalisation" of production to low wage countries via foreign direct investment, which could reduce demand for skilled labour; and increased international competition which could lead to investment in skilled-labour-intensive technologies. On the other hand, traditional theory implies a small impact, if any, of trade on the overall level of employment, by assuming away labour market rigidities and unsound policy responses to labour market problems.

Results in the empirical literature suggest, first, that the impact of trade on the labour market is very difficult to assess and, second, that trade has played only a small role in labour market outcomes, such as changes in relative employment and wages of unskilled labour in OECD countries (OECD, 1997*d*; European Commission, 1997*a*; Slaughter, 1998 and Wood, 1998). Due to data availability most studies concern the United States. Most studies concerning Europe do not find a significant impact of trade with low wage countries on the labour market (Cortes and Jean, 1995). On the contrary, trade and international competition among OECD countries seem to have played some role. Freeman and Revenga (1995) find for the OECD countries some moderate effects of import competition on employment and wages. As expected, they find that in Europe employment is more sensitive to imports than wages, while the opposite is true in the United States. Moreover they find evidence that the impact on employment of intra-OECD trade is more important than the impact of non-OECD trade. On the other hand, Neven and Wyplosz (1996) use import prices instead of trade flows as an indicator of international competitive pressure and they find that European industries are affected by competition with developing and developed countries to the same extent. Restructuring at the industry level, though, involves substantial defensive innovation accompanied by skills upgrading in the workforce, rather than reflecting the patterns of adjustment predicted by the Hecksher-Ohlin model. The authors find different results across the four European countries in the sample and suggest that the reason probably reflects differences in labour market legislation and functioning.

Another line of research is the literature on the impact of European integration on the economy, which takes into account employment effects. This has generally been assessed using both macro models and computable general equilibrium (CGE) models. The efficiency gains due to market integration are typically modelled via its impact on demand elasticities perceived by producers.[60] A reduction in firms' mark-ups is likely to have a positive impact on employment. Static models, such as in Mercenier (1995), find that although welfare effects are unambiguously positive for Europe the gains are quite modest. Taking into account growth effects can increase the size of the impact. The European Commission (1996*b*), for instance, estimated that the Single Market Programme generated 300 000 jobs by 1994.

Most of these studies, with few exceptions, limit their analysis to the unrealistic full-employment/flexible-wage case. European Commission (1996*b*) estimates, using a model which allows for unemployment, show a three-fold rise in the size of employment gains. In that exercise wages are set in a bargaining framework and trade unions are able to extract some monopoly rent from firms. A decrease in mark-ups has a negative effect on wage claims and it strengthens the employment effect. Mercenier (1995) introduces some short-run rigidities in his model and, contrary to the results obtained with the full-employment case, finds that welfare gains more than doubled in Europe, with five-fold increases in some cases. The author assumes that wages are tied to the consumer price index. Lower mark-ups, when translated into lower prices and wages, increase external competitiveness and boost output and employment. Instead of assuming costless entry and exit of firms, Burniaux and Waelbroeck (1997) take into account a potential side effect of the Single Market Program, that is the possibility that European labour markets have in fact failed to reallocate efficiently the factors released by the firms which close down. They suggest that large adjustment costs may arise if some of the workers belonging to firms closing down decide to retire definitively; and this is most likely in Europe where firms are more reluctant to hire older workers and generous retirement schemes may encourage workers to withdraw from the workforce. In their model the efficiency gains stemming from European integration are partially offset by the wastage of labour as older workers retire from the labour market.

IV. The future agenda

The European Union has lived long enough and is big enough to have had a sizeable impact on the multilateral trading system. However, it is difficult to draw general lessons because of the difficulty of sorting out what is generic and what is specific to the EU's history. Nonetheless, one lesson can be drawn: deep integration in Europe shows that a vast regional integration scheme does not necessarily undermine the multilateral system, and many observers have pointed out that the creation of the European Union and its enlargement provided an impetus to start multilateral negotiations. In addition, multilateral negotiations have benefited from the EU's internal integration experience as this often gave confidence that practical ways exist to tackle new trade issues.

Concerning the future, it is conceivable that the reduction of the number of independent middle-sized and small countries, which have the strongest interest in maintaining an open world trading system, could sow the seeds for more protectionist policies. The same could happen if the EU's success with deepening and widening led to the creation of trading blocs elsewhere, to the extent that these were inward looking. While an empirical assessment of such tendencies is impossible, recent theoretical advances point to a variety of possible outcomes (Box 6). However, the trade agenda of the Community for the coming years can shed some light on these questions.

Priorities in the Community's future trade agenda are:

- To strengthen co-operation on trade-related issues with major trading partners.
- To deepen integration with the eastern European and Mediterranean countries.
- To actively pursue multilateral liberalisation.

Co-operation on trade-related issues

Trade and competition

Since the foundation of the Community, a strong common competition policy was seen as important to ensure free and undistorted competition, as

Box 6. Welfare and the number of trading blocs

Since the mid-1980s, a fast growing body of economic research has accompanied the revival of regionalism. One of the key questions analysed is how world welfare is affected by the number of trading blocs. The traditional view held that world welfare decreases with the number of trade blocs, because in a world where every country forms its own bloc, welfare is minimised as every country levies tariffs on all foreign goods and services. On the other hand, world welfare increases as trade barriers are removed among the members of ever larger trading blocs, and finally, global free trade reigns.

While there is agreement that a world without trade barriers would maximise world welfare, the move towards large regional trading blocs may not procure a monotonic rise in welfare. Indeed, basic trading-bloc models (Krugman, 1991 and Frankel *et al.*, 1996) have shown that world welfare is U-shaped in the number of trading blocs and that the number of trading blocs that minimise welfare is small – as few as two or three. A world with only a few large trading blocs is harmful for two reasons: each of the large blocs will be tempted to use its monopoly power by raising tariffs to a greater extent than a smaller bloc would and the elimination of tariffs within blocs introduces more distortions than it eliminates. In view of current developments in the formation of regional trading blocs in Europe, America and Asia these results are not encouraging.

An important extension to this model is the explicit modelling of transport costs. If blocs were formed on a continental basis and intercontinental transport cost were prohibitive, then consolidation into continental blocs becomes the best outcome, because there is no intercontinental trade to be diverted. Krugman dubbed such regional blocs as "natural", because if blocs are formed by countries with low trading costs regionalism is a beneficial policy also in terms of world welfare. Trading costs are obviously not prohibitive, so that there will be a mapping between such costs and intra-bloc preference margins which will generate positive returns for regionalism (preferences are low as compared to transport cost) or negative returns (preferences are high as compared to transport cost).

Even more difficult to tackle are questions about the dynamics of regional trade agreements and their interaction with multilateralism (Bhagwati and Panagariya, 1996 and Winters, 1996): will they be "stumbling blocks" or "building blocks" towards worldwide trade liberalisation? Regional agreements have attracted many new members and defections are rare. Overall, these agreements appear to create a "domino" effect, as outsiders lose competitiveness and exporters will lobby for entry. New memberships could raise the cost of non-membership and pull in countries at the next margin. Sapir (1998) argues that the demand for regional trade agreements by the CEECs and the Mediterranean countries was strongly influenced by domino effects, while the supply of agreements by the Union was partly driven by the desire to gain discriminatory market access and to reinforce regional stability. The regional integration process could end up in global free trade and the path towards it could be accelerated further, if regional agreements provide an incentive to outsiders to conclude multilateral trade negotiations. While regional integration schemes have attracted new members, regionalism

Box 6. **Welfare and the number of trading blocs** *(cont.)*

has also provided an incentive to form new regional integration schemes, partly in order to create greater bargaining power. This can lead to multilateral free trade through continued expansion and coalescence of the regional agreements. But it may also lead to a fragmentation of the world economy as regional liberalisation could reduce the incentive to liberalise with the non-Member world. Inward-looking trading blocs or aggressive unilateralism could be the consequence. It should be stressed that these recent modelling efforts do often rely on assumptions that have little resemblance with reality. It is, for instance, often assumed that countries behave as "optimal tariff setters".

anti-competitive behaviour and subsidies can distort trade in the same way as border measures do. Outside the European Union, too, co-operation on competition policy matters has increasingly been seen as necessary to prevent anti-competitive practices, which could hurt EU companies. Therefore, the European Union has established competition policy co-operation agreements with a number of major trading partners.

The Commission's White Paper on the future integration of eastern European countries into the Community underlined the importance of a viable competition policy for economies in transition. These countries are currently in the process of developing competition laws modelled on EU rules, with technical assistance from the Commission. In order to identify potential problems in implementing Community law upon accession, screening meetings on the competition *acquis* were organised with the applicant countries (Cyprus, Czech Republic, Estonia, Hungary, Poland and Slovenia) in 1998 and in 1999 (with Bulgaria, Latvia, Lithuania, Romania and the Slovak Republic). However, competition rules are still judged to be in need of improvement in several countries and the competition chapter remains open mainly due to insufficient progress made in the field of state aid.

Similar provisions on competition are included in the agreements with the Mediterranean countries, even though accession for these countries is not on the table, except for Cyprus and Malta. Proposals for implementing rules are being prepared for Egypt, Tunisia, Israel, Jordan and the Palestinian Authority, and it is expected that these will be forwarded to the Community's Mediterranean partners in the course of 2000. Although progress is slow, the EU-Russia, EU-Ukraine and EU-Moldova Partnership and Co-operation Agreement Joint Committees have now established Subcommittees, with the task of overseeing the fulfilment of the commitments in the field of competition and state aid. The free trade agreements concluded in 1999 with South Africa and Mexico contain provisions concerning competition and state aid, including a mechanism for co-operation between the competition authorities.

The EU bilateral agreement with the United States is another example of competition policy co-operation. The main purpose of this agreement is the co-ordination of the application of competition laws. It contains a "positive comity" clause, which gives either party the right to request the other to act on the basis of its own powers, and to investigate activities which adversely affect important interests of the first party. The notified party is free to decide whether to undertake enforcement activities, but if it does so, it is obliged to advise the first party of the outcome. This "positive comity" clause was used for the first time in 1999 in a case involving access to computer airline reservation systems in Europe. EU investigations, at the request of the United States, led to the settlement between the US complainant and two European carriers, Lufthansa and Scandinavian Airways. The controversial merger between Boeing and McDonnell Douglas and controversy surrounding the proposed co-operation between British Airways and American Airlines underline the need for close co-operation in this area in order to avoid trade frictions and to provide for a fair assessment of cross-border spillovers of domestic and international mergers. On the other hand, it also shows that there is still a long way to go to create an institutional framework to handle such cases. Against this background, the United States and the European Union set up in 1999 a joint committee to discuss possible improvements to approval procedures for mergers and acquisitions having an impact on both sides of the Atlantic. The Commission also finalised discussions with Canada on a bilateral co-operation agreement, and an accord was signed in June 1999. The agreement essentially provides for the reciprocal notification of cases under investigation by either authority, the possibility of co-ordination by the two authorities of their enforcement activities and the possibility for one party to request the other to take enforcement action. Japan and the European Union have contacts via the Japanese Fair Trade Commission (JFTC). At their bilateral meeting in October 1999, the Commission presented a request for a broader and more rigorous application of Japanese competition rules. The EU request focused mainly on more effective enforcement of the Anti-monopoly Act (AMA) and on further suppression of exemptions and exceptions from the AMA.

In July 1995, the Commission published a report by a group of experts (the "van Miert Report"), which draws up proposals for strengthening international co-operation between the European Union and its trading partners in the field of competition policy in the years ahead.[61] It considered that a strengthened framework for co-operation between competition authorities and for an exchange of information is essential for achieving effective enforcement of competition rules. It also suggested that the international community needs to be equipped with the power to ensure that the authorities of the country in which offending firms are located act to eliminate the anti-competitive practice. A combination of several steps is recommended in order to limit anti-competitive practices, which have international effects. A first step would be to encourage countries or regional groupings of countries to ensure that they have an adequate set of competition rules in place, comprising agreed minimum standards, *per se* prohibitions and a rules of reason approach, and that these are effectively enforced. A second step would be a strengthening of existing bilateral comity-based agreements. A final step would be the negotiation of a plurilateral agreement including most of the elements already incorporated into the bilateral agreements, comprising a set of minimum competition rules and a binding positive comity instrument. An international body would oversee the agreement and its further development, establish a register of anti-competitive practices and provide a dispute settlement structure. This framework would include, in the first instance, a group of core countries only, although it should expand its coverage progressively in terms of its geographic scope, substantive coverage and surveillance.

In June 1996, the Commission published a Communication on Developing an International Framework for Competition Rules. The WTO is identified as the most suitable body to deal with multilateral competition rules. The report recommended the creation of a framework in which the WTO countries could eventually adopt and enforce their own competition rules along commonly adopted principles. Following a European initiative at the WTO ministerial meeting in Singapore in December 1996, a WTO Working Group on the interaction between trade and competition policy was created. The Group discusses the relevance of fundamental WTO principles of national treatment, transparency, and most-favoured-nation treatment for competition policy. Several approaches have been considered that promote co-operation and communication among members, including in the field of technical co-operation and the contribution of competition policy to achieving the objectives of the WTO. In preparation of the WTO Ministerial Conference in Seattle, the European Union tabled proposals for the launching of negotiations towards a multilateral framework of competition rules. They included three main elements: first, all WTO members should introduce basic competition rules and enforce them; second, core common principles should guarantee a degree of coherence and commonality between WTO members and third, co-operation between competition agencies in member countries should be possible through a multilateral instrument. Currently, no negotiations are taking place regarding trade and competition as no agreement was reached between the WTO members at the Seattle Ministerial Conference regarding the launch of a new round of multilateral trade negotiations. However, the WTO has continued its work on the interaction between trade and competition policy (WTO, 2000*b*).

Standardisation and certification

The Community's trade objectives regarding standards and conformity assessment are to eliminate or reduce TBTs in third countries and to encourage those countries to adopt standards based on, or compatible with, international and EU practices.[62] The strategy pursued is four-fold and relies simultaneously on: the WTO multilateral framework complemented with bilateral initiatives; the negotiation of mutual recognition agreements (MRAs); technical assistance programmes to developing countries to promote the adoption of international or European standards; and regulatory co-operation, whether multilateral, plurilateral, or bilateral, on some key industrial sectors such as vehicles, pharmaceuticals, medical equipment, foodstuffs and chemicals.

European initiatives concerning MRAs are based on three main conditions: the competence of the third country technical bodies, limitation of recognition to the activity of the designated bodies, and on achieving a balanced situation with regard to the advantages derived by both parties for the products concerned (WTO, 1996). Hence MRAs do not presuppose harmonisation of each party's substantive requirements or recognition of their equivalence (as with the EU's internal market). They require, though, full confidence in each side's certification process. In the case of the EEA and accession countries, mutual recognition is or will be based on common regulations, because the ultimate goal is full integration. In most other cases, however, MRAs will operate where the parties' underlying rules remain different. With the objective to implement the Community's *acquis* with regard to technical regulations for accession countries, negotiations with Hungary and the Czech Republic started in 1997 and negotiations with Poland are foreseen to start at the end of 2000 for European Conformity Assessment Agreements (ECAA). The main subjects of negotiation are standardisation, certification, accreditation and laws on safety of products and liability of manufacturers.

The Community has established MRAs on conformity assessment with the United States, Australia, New Zealand and Canada, and has initialled agreements with Switzerland and Israel. Standardisation plays an increasing role in the relationship between the United States and the Union. The US Department of Commerce estimates that EU legislation covering regulated products could affect 50 per cent of US exports to Europe.[63] Discussions between the United States and the European Union concerning MRAs in the areas of certification and testing procedures have been ongoing since October 1992 and the text of a new MRA was submitted for approval and implementation in June 1997. The final package, which entered into force on 1 December 1998, included information and telecommunication equipment, pharmaceutical goods, medical devices, electrical safety, electromagnetic compatibility and recreational crafts. MRAs between the European Union, Australia and New Zealand entered into force in January 1999. For the MRAs to be fully operational, Conformity Assessment Bodies (CABs) had to be designated. The first group of CABs was designated in March 1999 and a second group agreed upon in May for the MRA with Australia. The EU-New Zealand MRA covers telecommunication terminal equipment, low voltage electrical equipment, electromagnetic compatibility, machinery, pressure equipment, medical devices and pharmaceutical goods; and the EU-Australia MRA also covers motor vehicles. There is scope to expand the coverage of the MRA to new sectors over time (*e.g.* aircraft airworthiness). A MRA between the European Union and Canada entered into force in November 1998. The Agreement covers mandatory conformity procedures in the same sectors as the MRA with the United States, but also applies to radio transmitters. Current negotiations between the European Union and Japan cover pharmaceuticals, medical devices, telecommunications equipment and electrical equipment.

Reflecting growing consumer concerns, the desire to improve labelling and segregating the various food and feed ingredients, which may contain genetically modified organisms (GMOs) was high on the EU agenda. A new regulatory framework concerning the marketing of GMOs is under consideration. As of March 2000, 18 products, mainly modified soybeans, oil seed rape, and maize have been granted Community market access. No new authorisations were granted in 1999 or in 2000 to date. A mandatory labelling of food and food ingredients that include GMOs was established in April 2000. The European Union issued a White Paper in January 2000 proposing the establishment of an independent European Food Authority by 2002, with responsibilities for both risk assessment and communication on food safety issues. It establishes a timetable for more than eighty legislative measures for new or reformed food and feed-safety rules that are envisaged over the next few years. An organic-food labelling system, offering consumers the guarantee that the product concerned contains at least 95 per cent organic ingredients, was adopted.

The impact of different regulatory approaches in sensitive areas such as biotechnology and food safety also demonstrated the need for better bilateral and multilateral co-operation. A Transantlantic Economic Partnership (TEP) between the European Union and the United States was launched in May 1998 aiming in particular to remove regulatory barriers to trade in both goods and services by closer co-operation between regulators. It envisages negotiations of mutual recognition of technical regulations and professional qualifications. The plan proposes joint action and co-operation in the areas of consumer and plant health, biotechnology, environment and food safety. In particular, a joint exercise was launched to step-up efforts to better co-ordinate genetically modified food policies. Approval procedures will be compared and subsequently products will be submitted for approval simultaneously on both sides and regulators will be consulted throughout the process. In addition, a working group including scientists, farmers and possibly other representatives of civil society will provide consumer information about the safety of such products. A veterinary agreement between the European Union and the United States was signed in July 1999 with the objective of facilitating trade in live animals and meat by establishing a mechanism for the recognition of equivalence of sanitary measures operating in the two regions. The Commission has conducted negotiations with a number of other countries. Agreements have been concluded with New Zealand, Canada and the Czech Republic. Negotiations are continuing with Australia, Uruguay, Chile and Argentina.

Trade and investment

The liberalisation of capital movements was an objective of the Union from the outset and largely achieved with the 1988 Directive on capital movements. By the early 1990s, capital controls had been removed in all EU countries. A few remaining restrictions concern FDI in certain sectors (typically transport and communications), acquisition of real estate by foreigners for non-business purposes and admission of certain securities issued by non-EU residents. The restrictions are motivated by industrial policy, sovereignty and prudential concerns. The Maastricht Treaty went a step further, by prohibiting restrictions on capital movements and on payments also between Member States and third countries. However, restrictions on direct investment, on the provision of financial services or on the admission of securities to capital markets existing at the end of 1993 could be maintained.

At the Singapore Conference in December 1996, the WTO set up a working group on the relationship between trade and investment. The group engaged in an intense debate on whether investment should be incorporated in the next round of WTO negotiations. The Union believes that international rules on FDI should be based on the fundamental WTO principles of non-discrimination, a "level playing field", as well as transparency and openness (in its view, the WTO provides the best forum to achieve this) and that negotiations on FDI in a new trade round should cover access to investment opportunities, protection of investment and rights to regulate, investors' responsibilities and sustainable development. Fairly ambitious negotiations at the OECD on a Multilateral Agreement on Investment (MAI) that would have replaced the current network of bilateral agreements and that also included a number of developing countries, failed in 1998.

Deepening regional integration

Regional agreements and the GATT's *Article* XXIV

Since the start of European integration and more recently again in the WTO, countries outside EU preferential agreements asked legitimately whether their interests would be hurt by the rising number of regional agreements. Such concerns do obviously not only apply to EU arrangements but are an inherent possible problem in any free trade agreement. GATT rules on customs unions and free trade areas do attempt to ensure that third country interests are respected and that they are compatible with a rules based and progressively more open world trading system. Article XXIV of the GATT, for instance, states that agreements must free "substantially all trade" and that trade barriers with respect to third countries must not be higher on the whole than prior to the agreement.

However, the interpretation of the GATT provisions has always been difficult. The GATT contracting parties could never reach an agreement on whether the original EC Treaty is consistent with Article XXIV. Such disagreements have continued since then, in relation to EU regional agreements as well as other preferential agreements.[64] On the other hand, despite problems of compatibility with GATT rules, preferential treatment has only seldom been the subject of dispute settlement proceedings.[65] The WTO is currently considering whether reforms in this area are necessary. In this context, several developments concerning EU agreements should be noted:

- Recent agreements provide for reciprocal industrial free trade areas over short transition periods; agricultural trade is also covered, even though liberalisation is still much less ambitious[66] than for industrial goods; and many agreements also provide for liberalisation of trade in services.
- The European Union encourages countries which are party to a preferential EU agreement to join the WTO, to liberalise trade unilaterally and to form free trade agreements among themselves.
- In 1995, the Council established that the Commission has to produce studies on the conformity with WTO provisions and the impact on common policies of each new preferential agreement proposal.

The risk of trade diversion is, nevertheless, real in the context of the eastern European and Mediterranean Agreements. This is also true for free trade agreements elsewhere. Indeed, the European Union itself is pushing for reform of WTO procedures in order to increase the legal certainty for its own preferential agreements and in order not to suffer from trade distortions from preferential agreements being struck elsewhere. European Commission (1996*c*), for instance, points to trade diversion in the context of NAFTA, the free trade area that was formed by countries where one or more of the partners had comparatively high duties on imports from the European Union, but zero duties exist on trade within the free trade area. Yeats (1997) came to a similar conclusion for the Latin American MERCOSUR agreement.

Relations with central and eastern European countries

An increasing number of countries in this region have identified EU membership as vital for the achievement of economic growth and political and social development. The European Union has received applications for membership from ten central and eastern European countries (CEECs). In March 1998, the first wave of accession negotiations was formally launched with Hungary, Poland, the

Czech Republic, Slovenia, and Estonia. In the wake of the Kosovo crisis, the Commission took a further step towards expanding the European Union when it proposed in October 1999 to open such negotiations with Latvia, Lithuania and the Slovak Republic, and on a conditional basis, with Bulgaria and Romania.

The first step towards future EU enlargement involved the negotiation of Europe Agreements (EAs). They form the institutional framework for trade integration between the CEECs and the European Union and govern economic aid and political co-operation between the European Union and the applicant countries. EAs have been concluded between the European Union and Poland, Hungary, the Czech Republic, Slovak Republic, Romania, Slovenia, and Bulgaria. Lithuania, Latvia and Estonia are in the process of being associated. The EAs are fully implemented only after ratification by the national parliaments and the European parliament. The trade provisions of the EAs, called the Interim Agreements[67] (IA), have however been implemented in each of the CEECs (Table 15).

The main objectives of these agreements are the creation of bilateral free trade areas for non-agricultural products within a period of ten years, close compatibility of economic laws and practice, and the development of a framework for political dialogue and economic co-operation. The EAs also commit the CEECs to approximate competition rules, intellectual property rights, banking law, nuclear law, transport and environment laws, right of establishment, and to ensure compliance with international agreements such as the WTO. These commitments have formed the basis of pre-accession strategies of applicant countries.

The basic liberalisation principles embodied in the EAs are preferential treatment, asymmetric reductions in tariffs and the respect of rules of origin. The European Union committed itself to a liberalisation schedule that is faster than for the other countries with the elimination of all quotas and levies on industrial

Table 15. **Europe Agreements**

Country	WTO member	Agreement in force	Interim agreement on trade with EU
Hungary	Yes	February 1994	March 1992
Poland	Yes	February 1994	April 1992
Czech Republic	Yes	October 1995	April 1992
Slovak Republic	Yes	February 1995	April 1992
Bulgaria	Yes	February 1995	December 1994
Romania	Yes	February 1995	December 1994
Estonia	Yes	Pending ratification	January 1995
Latvia	Yes	Pending ratification	January 1995
Lithuania	Accession requested	Pending ratification	January 1995
Slovenia	Yes	February 1999	June 1996

Source: European Commission and WTO.

goods imported from the CEECs with the exception of steel and textiles as soon as the IAs were in force. The European Union removed all quantitative restrictions on imports of textile and clothing products on 1 January 1998. The EA countries are to complete their bilateral liberalisation schedules by 2001 for the Czech Republic, Hungary, Lithuania, the Slovak Republic, Slovenia and by 2002 for Bulgaria, Latvia, Poland and Romania. Trade liberalisation concerned only products originating either in the European Union or in CEEC's until 1997, when a European-wide diagonal rule of origin system was introduced (see above).

Table 16 gives an overview of CEEC MFN tariffs in comparison with the EU average. In 1996, the CEECs were still considerably more protectionist than the European Union. As noted above, the difference between the MFN and preferential tariffs of the members of a preferential trade agreement can have important implications for trade. Messerlin (1996) has calculated differences between the highest MFN tariffs of the CEECs and the European Union for each ISIC three-digit sector and found that the highest tariffs in these countries are often 20 percentage points higher than the corresponding EU tariffs. On the other hand, agricultural protection is considerably higher in the European Union than in the CEECs, and

Table 16. **Eastern European and Baltic MFN tariffs**

1996, per cent

	MFN tariff, unweighted averages				Output-weighted tariff averages[2]
	All goods	Processed food sectors	Manufacturing[1]	Sensitive sectors	
Founding members of CEFTA[3]					
Czech Republic	8.0	19.0	5.9	7.2	. .
Hungary	10.0	10.4	10.1	10.9	10.2
Poland	10.3	18.3	8.4	9.0	21.2
Slovak Republic	10.0	22.3	7.6	9.6	10.3
Founding members of BFTA[4]					
Estonia	. .	. .	. .	. .	. .
Latvia	9.9	14.6	9.4	8.4	10.6
Lithuania	4.5	14.1	2.6	5.5	8.0
Other EEBCs[5]					
Romania	10.3	15.6	9.1	10.1	11.6
Slovenia	29.0	28.9	24.8	24.7	. .
Other countries					
EU	7.2	16.0	6.6	8.1	. .

1. Only non-sensitive sectors.
2. Output-weighted tariffs, for 3-digit ISIC industrial sectors.
3. CEFTA: Central European Free Trade Agreement.
4. BFTA: Baltic Free Trade Agreement.
5. EEBC: Eastern European and Baltic countries.

Source: Messerlin (1996).

the EAs do not provide for liberalisation in this area. The OECD's (2000*b*) calculations of Producer Support Estimates show that in 1999, the average value of market support was 49 per cent of the value of production for the European Union as a whole. This contrasts with much lower levels of protection of 25 per cent in the Czech Republic and Poland and 20 per cent in Hungary.

Some of these trade issues are likely to disappear as soon as accession negotiations are completed. In 1997, the Commission submitted its opinions on individual applications and provided a communication on the future financial framework to cope with enlargement (European Commission, 1997*b*). The major challenges facing the Community are the large differences between applicant countries and the European Union, as well as the fact that all of them will be net recipients of Community funds. In addition, institutional reforms of the European Union that should have been achieved via the Amsterdam Treaty (such as the reweighting of the votes in the Council, and the reduction of the number of Commissioners), and which were seen as necessary for enlargement, did not live up to expectations.

On the other hand, progress has been made in implementing the accession agenda. Applicant countries were screened by the Commission on the basis of political criteria (democratic rules, rule of law, etc.), economic criteria (functioning of the market economy) and their ability to take on the obligations of membership, including adherence to the aims of political, economic and monetary union. Based on an extensive analysis, the Commission concluded that the Council should open accession negotiations with the ten CEEC countries mentioned above. The 1999 annual report on each of the 13 candidate countries (European Commission, 1999) on the progress towards accession highlighted the economic and legislative reforms undertaken in the CEECs but also underlined the necessity for further adjustments. Moreover, an intergovernmental EU conference, which started in February 2000, will have the task of reviewing the size and composition of the Commission, the weighting of votes in the Council and other amendments needed to prepare the European Union for enlargement. From the end of 2002 onwards, the European Union could admit the first applicant countries that have shown themselves capable of assuming the obligations deriving from accession, even though no deadlines have been set. In the meantime, the free movement of labour following accessions has become a major contentious issue in some EU countries. Moreover, some of the new obligations for accession countries could be so exacting that long transition periods are being considered. This is particularly so for agriculture, where first-order social changes are implied, as well as for infrastructure and the environment, where massive investments may be needed. Progress as regards the capacity to implement the *acquis* is monitored in an annual report submitted by the Commission to the Council.

In this context, of considerable importance are also the financial implications of the enlargement on the Community budget. In March 1999, the European

Table 17. **The EU's new financial framework**

Billion €, 1999 prices

	2000	2001	2002	2003	2004	2005	2006
Appropriations for commitments	**92.0**	**93.5**	**94.0**	**93.2**	**91.7**	**91.1**	**90.7**
Agriculture	40.9	42.8	43.9	43.8	42.8	41.9	41.7
Structural Funds and Cohesion Fund	32.0	31.5	30.9	30.3	29.6	29.6	29.2
Internal policies	5.9	6.0	6.2	6.3	6.4	6.5	6.6
External action	4.6	4.6	4.6	4.6	4.6	4.6	4.6
Administration	4.6	4.6	4.7	4.8	4.9	5.0	5.1
Reserves	0.9	0.9	0.7	0.4	0.4	0.4	0.4
Pre-accession aid for applicant countries	3.1	3.1	3.1	3.1	3.1	3.1	3.1
Appropriations for payments							
New Member States after accession	..	..	4.1	6.7	8.9	11.4	14.2
Total ceiling	89.6	91.1	98.4	101.6	100.8	101.6	103.8
Total ceiling (as a % of GNP)	1.13	1.12	1.18	1.19	1.15	1.13	1.13

Source: European Commission (2000), "Europe's Agenda 2000: Strengthening and widening the European Union".

Council reached an overall agreement on a financial framework extending through 2006 (Agenda 2000). It suggests that the current budgetary ceiling on own resources (1.2 per cent of EU GNP) may not have to be lifted (Table 17). Concerning the Structural Funds, this would imply a freeze of nominal expenditure for the EU15 at € 30 billion annually, a reduction in the number of Objectives from seven to three (two regional and one human resource related), a streamlining of the number of programmes, and a strict application of thresholds. On the other hand, the Cohesion Fund will be maintained in its present form in the short run but a review of eligibility will be undertaken at mid-term. For agriculture, annual spending of close to € 40 billion is foreseen. Agricultural spending will be capped in real terms, underpinned by the CAP reforms outlined above. Regarding enlargement, the underlying assumption is that new members would join from 2002 onwards. Expenditure related to pre-accession (€ 3.1 billion per annum) and accession (rising from € 4.1 billion in 2002 to € 14.2 billion in 2006) is ring-fenced, *i.e.* cannot be appropriated for other purposes.

Relations with the Confederation of Independent States

The European Union has signed Partnership and Co-operation Agreements (PCA) with Russia, Ukraine, Belarus, Azerbaijan, Armenia, Georgia, Kazakhstan, Kyrgyzstan, Uzbekistan and Moldova. A PCA between the European Union and the Former Yugoslav Republic of Macedonia was initialled in June 1996. In early 1997, the Council of Ministers gave the Commission a mandate to start negotiations with Turkmenistan to conclude a PCA (Table 18). They replace the Trade

Table 18. **Partnership and Co-operation Agreements**

Country	Export and import controls	WTO member	PCA Agreement signed	Interim agreement on trade in force
Russia	Export tariffs on oil increased in January 2000 to €15 per tonne. Some exported goods are subject to self-restraints under PCA. Some products are subject to quotas. In 1999, maximum tariff rate was 30% (exception on strong alcoholic beverages 100%). Import duties reduced to 20% on cars, tobacco, some clothes and precious stones. Import quotas applied to vodka and pure spirit. Customs fee of 0.15% applies to all products imported.	Accession requested	June 1994	July 1995
Ukraine	In 1999, the number of imported items exempt from VAT until 2001 was lowered from over 200 to 48. A uniform 2% import surcharge was imposed for 6 months from July 1999. Various permits and licences are still required to engage in foreign trade. Averaged weighted duty was 7.5% in 1999. Seasonal tariffs apply to agricultural products. 50% export revenue surrender requirement introduced after the Russian crisis, remains. Export licences and duties apply to certain products.	Accession requested	June 1994	June 1995
Belarus	Since late 1998, duties have been in force on imports and transit of oil and oil products. Strict price regulations.	Accession requested	March 1995	March 1995
Azerbaijan	NA	Accession requested	March 1996	July 1999
Armenia	NA	Accession requested	Initialled December 1995	April 1996
Georgia	Base rate of tariffs is 12%, 5% for capital goods and 25% for agriculture products.	Accession requested	March 1996	July 1999
Kazakstan	Protectionist measures introduced in 1999 as a result of the Russian crisis are still in place.	Accession requested	January 1995	May 1996
Kyrgyzstan	Uniform tariff rate of 10% applies to imports.	Yes	February 1994	
Uzbekistan	Highly protectionist measures introduced in 1999 as a result of the Russian crisis still in place. Additional fees for customs formalities are charged. Some import prohibitions exist. State monopoly for export of cotton and gold, export surrender increased to 50%.	Accession requested	June 1996	July 1999

Table 18. **Partnership and Co-operation Agreements** (*cont.*)

Country	Export and import controls	WTO member	PCA Agreement signed	Interim agreement on trade in force
Moldova	WTO compatible laws regulating imports passed in 1999.	Accession requested	Pending November 1994	
Turkmenistan	Some price controls remain in effect. Few tariff and non-tariff barriers exist. Foreign trade is constrained through restrictions on access to foreign exchange.	No	Initialled May 1997	
Former Yugoslav Republic of Macedonia	NA	Accession requested	Initialled June 1996	

Source: European Commission.

and Co-operation Agreement of 1989 between the European Union and the Soviet Union and cover in particular the following areas: political dialogue; trade in goods (on the basis of MFN treatment); provisions affecting business and investment; cross-border supply of services; payment and capital; intellectual, industrial and commercial property protection; and economic co-operation in many areas. These agreements are valid for ten years, once they have been finally ratified. Interim Agreements have been signed and entered into force in order to provisionally apply the trade and trade-related provisions of the PCAs with Russia, Ukraine, Belarus and Moldova. Moreover, the European Union concluded an agreement on trade, commercial and economic co-operation with Mongolia, which provides for the countries to grant each other MFN treatment.

Euro-Mediterranean Agreements

Traditionally, the European Union has sought to strengthen its relations with its southern Mediterranean neighbours through a series of bilateral agreements. The Euro-Mediterranean Partnership represents a new direction by adding a multilateral forum for developing closer political and economic links in the area. The EU trading partners represented about half of the Mediterranean market over the 1990s. By contrast, the Mediterranean zone accounts for a small share of EU trade, roughly 3 per cent. An analysis by product shows that trade relations have been characterised by an important deficit in the energy sector, that was more than offset by surpluses on manufactured products, in particular transport equipment and machinery (Figure 8).

The Euro-Mediterranean partnership was formally established at the Barcelona Conference in November 1995. At this meeting, representatives of the EU Member States and the governments of Algeria, Cyprus, Egypt, Israel, Lebanon, Malta, Morocco, Syria, Tunisia, Jordan, Turkey and the Palestinian Authority unanimously adopted the Barcelona Declaration. The declaration has three principal dimensions: a political and security partnership, an economic and financial partnership, and partnership in social, cultural and human affairs. The second section of the declaration supports the creation of a free trade area by 2010 through the completion of the Euro-Mediterranean Association agreements (EMAs).[68] The third Euro-Mediterranean conference held in Stuttgart in April 1999 reaffirmed the priorities established at the Barcelona Conference with a view to improving in particular intra-regional and sub-regional co-operation and the participation of non-governmental institutions in the activities undertaken. The European Parliament recommended involving those Mediterranean third countries not currently participating in the Barcelona process, including Libya. At the bilateral level, the European Union has signed EMAs with Tunisia, Israel and Morocco and the Palestinian Authority. Similar agreements are still being negotiated with Egypt, Jordan and Lebanon. As with the eastern European countries, accession negotiations have

Figure 8. **Trade of the Mediterranean partners**[1]

A. Direction
1991-99 average

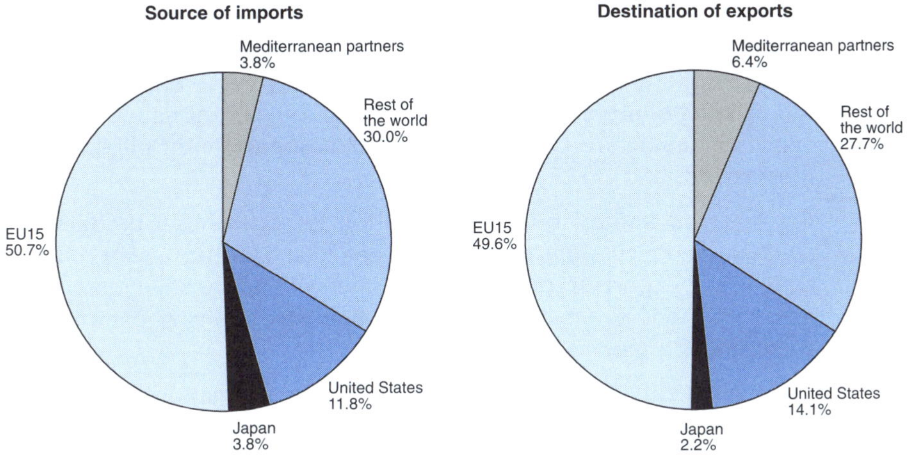

B. Composition
Total trade, 1990-96 average

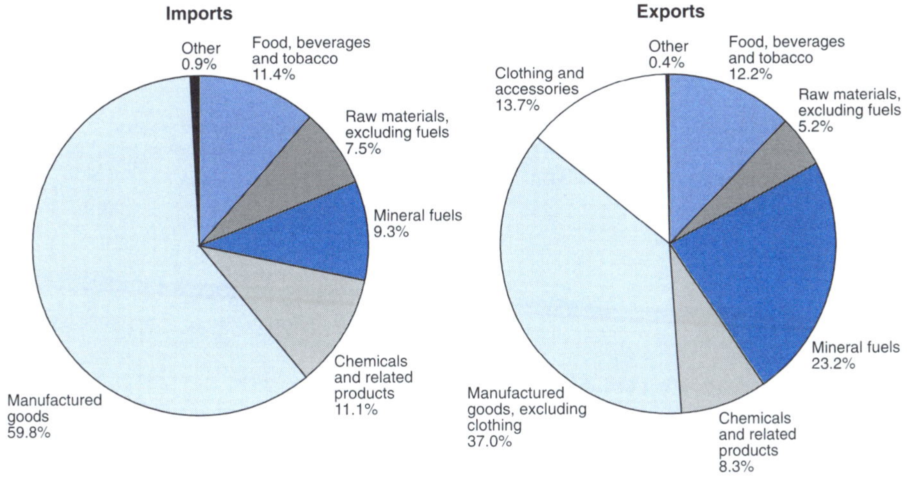

1. Algeria, Cyprus, Egypt, Israel, Jordan, Lebanon (Panel A only), Morocco, Syrian Arab Republic, Tunisia and Turkey.

Source: IMF, Direction of Trade Statistics, May 2000; United Nations (1999), *International Trade Statistics Yearbook 1996,* Volume I and OECD estimates.

started with Cyprus and Malta and the Commission proposed to consider also Turkey as an accession candidate. The latter entered into a customs union with the European Union in 1996.

The main features of the EMAs are the following (Table 19):

- Progressive elimination of all tariffs on industrial goods over 12 years. However, most manufactured exports from these countries already receive preferential customs treatment both by virtue of the GSP and of the existing bilateral agreements, whereas the current heavy protection against manufactured imports from the European Union will have to be dismantled.
- Gradual and limited trade liberalisation for agricultural products with substantive discussions only by the year 2000. Mediterranean countries' agricultural exports to the European Union will not receive more favourable treatment in the short run, with some exceptions where additional preferences are envisaged.
- Concerning services, EMAs simply refer to the obligations of each party under the GATS. Mediterranean countries made very limited commitments under the GATS.
- Measures to liberalise the right of establishment do not go beyond WTO commitments except for Lebanon.
- The EMAs envisage the adoption and application of the basic EU competition rules, a progressive elimination of non-tariff barriers, and harmonisation of safeguard and anti-dumping provisions within five years.

Table 19. **The Euro-Mediterranean Association agreements**[1]

Euro-Mediterranean Agreements (EMA)	
Tunisia	EMA signed July 1995
Israel	EMA signed November 1995
Morocco	EMA signed November 1995
Egypt	EMA being negotiated
Jordan	EMA being negotiated
Lebanon	EMA being negotiated
Palestinian Authority	EMA signed
Relations with neighbouring countries	
Turkey	Customs union entered into force January 1996,[2] negotiations for EU accession
Cyprus	Free trade area entered into force June 1973, negotiations for EU accession

1. All countries are WTO members except for Lebanon and the Palestinian Authority.
2. On 1 January 1996, Turkey adopted the EU Common Customs Regime (including the EU's common external tariff).
Source: WTO, 2000*a*.

During the transition period WTO rules with respect to countervailing duties and anti-dumping legislation will remain applicable. State aid for disadvantaged regions would have to be compatible with EU competition rules. EMAs generally refer to commitments of the Agreement on Trade Related Aspects of Intellectual Property rights (TRIPs). For non-WTO members, the legal framework would have to comply with WTO requirements both in terms of scope and enforcement with a transition period envisaged. Even though in principle Mediterranean countries already have duty-free access to EU markets for manufactured goods, in practice rules of origin may be such as to require the use of EU inputs in order to benefit from duty-free treatment.[69]

Furthermore, the absence of binding commitments in the areas of FDI and supply of services, the exclusion of government procurement and the maintenance of anti-dumping and broadly worded safeguard provisions imply that the EMAs do not go significantly beyond existing multilateral (WTO) disciplines.

The Commission considers that a substantial increase in financial support for the Mediterranean countries is necessary to achieve the objectives of its Mediterranean policy. Financial support should aim at helping the process of economic modernisation and restructuring of those countries prepared to open their markets in the context of new EMAs and support structural adjustment in countries less advanced in this process with a view to preparing them for entering into free trade with the Union. The Community's financial support will also focus on the strengthening of north-south economic and financial co-operation, and among southern and eastern Mediterranean countries themselves. For the 1995-99 period, € 4.9 billion were given in grants from the Community budget, plus loans from the European Investment Bank. By comparison, for the CEECs, an envelope of € 6.7 billion was granted.

Several studies have analysed the welfare implications of the trade agreements for a number of Mediterranean countries that have already concluded agreements. Rutherford *et al.* (1995) estimate that Morocco and Tunisia would experience welfare gains equivalent to around 1½ and 4½ per cent of GDP per year, respectively. The benefits would rise further in the event of MFN liberalisation on a multilateral basis to 2½ per cent of GDP a year for Morocco and 5¼ per cent for Tunisia. On the other hand, in the case of Tunisia, Brown *et al.* (1997) suggest that overall welfare could actually decline, due to the sizeable fall in tariff revenues.

In these countries, the reliance on customs tariffs for government revenue is high. The high level of tariffs raises several issues. There is again a risk of trade diversion. In addition, the higher the share of tariffs in total government revenues, the more difficult it may be to mobilise the alternative resources needed to allow a reduction in MFN tariffs on top of the implementation of the EMA. Moreover, manufactured goods with relatively high tariffs constitute a large share of imports from the European Union, so that the loss in customs revenues would be comparatively larger. Estimates from the *Centre d'études prospectives et d'informations internationales* (CEPII) point to fiscal losses of 1.4 per cent of GDP for Egypt, 1.5 per cent for Algeria, 2.9 per cent for Morocco and 6.0 per cent for Tunisia.

Revenue losses could also depend on the phasing of the liberalisation measures and the products affected. The strategy of starting with products that have the lowest tariffs is designed to reduce the fiscal adjustment costs. However, this strategy may entail sizeable welfare losses because the sectors receiving the highest protection at the outset would receive even higher protection in relative terms. Hoekman and Djankov (1995) argue that multilateral liberalisation could prove more difficult due to the revenue losses entailed by liberalisation *vis-à-vis* the European Union and the pressures by domestic and EU firms to maintain sheltered home markets, pressures that could be heightened by erroneous sequencing. In addition, the Uruguay Round Agreement on Agriculture will have important repercussions on agricultural trade of the Mediterranean countries with the European Union. Many Mediterranean countries depend heavily on food imports, the prices of which could increase following further liberalisation of agricultural trade. While higher prices will hurt consumers, farmers who could not compete with subsidised exports from OECD countries should benefit.

A Partnership Agreement will replace the Fourth Lomé Convention

The Fourth Lome Convention expired in February 2000. A Partnership Agreement between African, Caribbean and Pacific (ACP) States and the European Union entered into force on 1 March 2000 and was signed in Suva, Fiji in June 2000. The European Union grants duty-free treatment on industrial and processed agricultural products originating in 70 ACP countries on a non-reciprocal basis. The European Union and the ACP have requested a waiver that would roll over the existing trade preferences for a duration of eight years, by which time new WTO compatible trading arrangements are to be concluded.

Trade agreement with South Africa

The European Union concluded a trade, development and co-operation agreement with South Africa in March 1999, which entered into force on a provisional basis on 1 January 2000. Under this agreement, 95 per cent of EU imports from South Africa will be fully liberalised in ten years, and 86 per cent of South Africa's imports from the European Union will be fully liberalised in 12 years, covering, thus, more than 90 per cent of combined trade.

Relations with North America

The New Transatlantic Agenda (NTA) signed in 1995 in Madrid by the United States and the European Union commits the two partners to co-operate in a large number of political and economic areas. In the trade field the United States and the European Union agreed to work together to strengthen the multilateral trading system and to support the WTO. The main objective of the NTA is the establishment of a "New Transatlantic Market Place" designed to eliminate trade barriers that hinder the flows of goods, services and capital across the Atlantic. Initiatives which are being pursued in the framework of the Transatlantic Marketplace include: the negotiation of a customs co-operation and mutual assistance agreement covering simplification of customs procedures, data and personnel exchanges and increased investigative co-operation (this agreement was signed in 1996); the negotiation of a Mutual Recognition Agreement on standards certification covering various sectors (telecommunications equipment, pharmaceuticals, medical devices, recreational craft); the negotiation of a new agreement in the area of competition law enforcement which is intended to improve co-operation by complementing the 1991 Agreement between the United States and the European Union regarding the application of their competition laws, without replacing existing law, which does differ considerably; and regulatory co-operation seeking to make regulators more aware of the trade and investment consequences of their decisions and to discourage the development of divergent regulations that could otherwise become the source of future trade disputes.

Co-operation is also multilateral. This was, for instance, the case in the negotiation of the Information and Technology Agreement (ITA), which committed the two parties to attempt to conclude an ITA that will eliminate tariffs in the information technology sector by the year 2000. A provisional agreement between the Transatlantic partners and other WTO Members was reached at the WTO Singapore Ministerial meeting in December 1996 and finalised in the spring of 1997.

A major test for the NTA came in March 1996 with the adoption of the Helms-Burton Act[70] in the United States. The European Union is firmly opposed to the use of extraterritorial legislation by the US government and has challenged the Act before the WTO. The European Union has also adopted legislation making it illegal for European companies or individuals to comply with the Helms-Burton Act. A Regulation and a joint action were formally adopted in November 1996, giving the European Union a legal framework to defend interests which may be threatened by the act.

Concerning trade in goods and services, liberalisation between the United States and the European Union will continue on an MFN basis and the NTA does not provide for the creation of a free trade area. Close co-operation in a large number of areas, which are not yet well-defined under WTO rules, could help reduce trade frictions, and joint initiatives could boost liberalisation in the multilateral context. The Transatlantic Economic Partnership that aims at removing regulatory barriers, discussed above, is an example of close co-operation.

Efforts towards deeper integration in North America extend beyond the United States. In December 1997, Mexico and the European Union signed the Economic Partnership, Political Co-ordination and Co-operation Agreement. The agreement covers economic and commercial co-operation and political co-ordination. Concerning trade, the objective was to establish a free trade area, by gradually eliminating barriers to trade in goods and services, increase investment opportunities, provide adequate protection for intellectual property rights, and establish disciplines in areas such as government procurement and dispute settlement, among others. A free trade agreement was signed in March 2000 between Mexico and the European Union crowning an ambitious trade liberalisation agenda with a country outside Europe or the Mediterranean. The provisions on goods entered into force on 1 July 2000. EU exports to Mexico will be granted similar treatment to that enjoyed by the United States and Canada, implying an immediate lifting of duties on 47 per cent of EU exports. Remaining tariffs will be reduced to a maximum of 5 per cent by 2003. All duties will disappear at the latest by 2007. The European Union has waived the duties it charges on 82 per cent of Mexican industrial goods. The remaining will enter the EU market duty-free as of January 2003. Concerning agriculture, total liberalisation is expected in 2010. The agreement also liberalises significantly services and procurement over the next ten years. Meanwhile, relations with countries of Latin America took a new dimension with a first summit in Rio de Janeiro in June 1999. Leaders from the European Union, Chile, the MERCOSUR countries and the countries of Central America signed a framework agreement, the major aim of which is the development of a free-trade agreement by 2005.

The multilateral agenda

The European Union played a key role in the recent negotiations on basic telecommunications and on information technology. The WTO Declaration on Trade in Information Technology Products, for instance, provides for the elimination of customs duties and charges on information technology products by the year 2000, on an MFN basis. The agreement will cover well over 90 per cent of trade in such products. As the European Union is the second largest importer of information technology products in the world, the agreement represents a significant market access improvement for foreign suppliers. Strong EU support was also key for concluding the financial services agreement in December 1997.

It is obviously impossible to say much currently about the future negotiation stance of the European Union sector by sector and on trade-related issues. However, the European Union has reiterated on several occasions that a key part of its approach to external trade policies remains its commitment to further multilateral liberalisation under the umbrella of the WTO. It is committed to the framework for further liberalisation, which was already established when the WTO was set up and supports the additional decisions taken at the WTO Ministerial Conference in Singapore. The latter include the establishment of WTO work programmes on aspects of investment, competition and government procurement policies. The EU's vision concerning competition policy in a global setting has been laid out above. Concerning investment, the European Union considers that work in this area should be undertaken by the WTO's Group on investment. The European Union sees public procurement as another important area for further liberalisation and is committed to improve the WTO's Government Procurement Agreement by extending its membership and coverage.

Following up on the initiatives agreed upon in Singapore in 1996, the Community has put forward options to improve market access for the least developed countries (LDCs). In the short term, the Community has levelled EU preferences granted to LDC's to match the best available under the GSP and the Lomé Convention (except for certain sensitive products). In addition, it will simplify the rules of origin and extend the possibilities of accumulation for LDC's. Further revisions will depend on the development of market access arrangements with the ACP countries after a new agreement has been struck (see above). In the long term, the European Union supports the creation of a multilateral scheme of preferential market access in the context of a new round of world trade negotiations.

While the European Union has strongly supported the sectoral negotiations on telecommunications, information technology and financial services, it sees limits to the progress which can be achieved on an *ad hoc* or sectoral basis and does not want to have the debate on trade questions conducted in a fragmented manner and on a sectoral basis. It prefers package deals, allowing for comprehensive and broad liberalisation. This would enable participants in trade negotiations to take a broad view of their economic and other interests, provide for room to exploit the trade-offs inherent in such negotiations, and make it easier to explain the overall benefits of trade liberalisation to political constituencies.

Despite intensive preparations, efforts to consolidate and reconcile more than 200 proposals by WTO members failed and the third WTO Ministerial Conference in Seattle in late 1999 did not launch, as expected, a new round of multilateral liberalisation. The disagreements did not only concern specific issues that member countries wanted to see addressed but also the fundamental question on whether to launch a new round of trade negotiations at all. However, members remained committed to begin negotiations on further liberalisation of agriculture and services. While most members did support a further reduction of tariffs in the non-agricultural sector, a wide range of views prevailed with respect to negotiations covering labour standards, competition, investment, procurement, environmental rules and electronic commerce. Moreover, many developing countries questioned what they could gain from further liberalisation of trade unless the agenda of the next round fully reflected their concerns and interests and conditioned their support for negotiations in other areas on prior or parallel action to address these concerns. No date was set for resuming the talks, but the WTO was charged with designing procedural rules that would ensure transparency of the negotiating process and to conduct consultations to bridge differences on issues on which consensus is lacking (WTO, 2000*b*).

Following the Ministerial Conference in Seattle, the Commission reiterated that it is still aiming for a broad agenda in a new multilateral trade round and that it would aim at an early start (Lamy, 2000). Moreover, the WTO should update and improve its rules in response to globalisation and developing countries would need to be better integrated into the system and have freer market access. The European Union, for instance, participated in the confidence building package extending duty free access for essentially all least developed country imports, which the Quad group forwarded in March 2000 for consideration in the WTO in the hope of enticing developing countries to join a new round. A new round could enhance welfare in the European Union and elsewhere considerably. An EU study (Nagarajan, 1999) estimated that cuts in protection of 20 and 50 per cent would lead to worldwide annual welfare gains of US$220 and US$400 billion, respectively. If a new round would lead to a cut in protection by 50 per cent, the welfare gain would be twice as large as the OECD's estimate of the gains from the Uruguay Round. The gain for the European Union would be between US$50 and US$100 billion. An agreement on trade and competition that would lead to a modest reduction in collusion by 10 per cent would add another US$85 billion worldwide.

As civil society further engaged in domestic trade policy debates recently, the European Union has intensified the dialogue with non-governmental organisations (NGO). The European Union's main objective is to set a new approach to the dialogue with civil society representatives and NGOs on issues such as the environment, development, consumers' rights and business. In April 2000, the Trade Directorate of the Commission proposed a structure for the organisation of the dialogue with NGOs. It includes the continuation of the general meetings (twice per year) as opportunities to meet with the Trade Directorate and the Commissioner and present their views on overall trade and WTO initiatives of the European Union. The creation of issues groups to discuss specific topics such as trade and health issues, services, agriculture and the environment could be launched first. Discussion at a second stage could include investment, competition, WTO reform/transparency and regional trade policy issues. A contact group, based on the advisors who had been part of the Community Delegation to Seattle, would continue to function as liaison and sounding board, to facilitate the dialogue. The trade dialogue proposal received broad support from NGOs. Moreover, to build confidence among the public in the multilateral trading system, the European Union has made proposals for greater transparency and institutional reform of the WTO.

The social and environmental dimension of increased international trade has led to a heated debate in recent years, including the question whether trade policies should be used to pursue changes in standards in other countries. There is a clear case for regional or international co-operation concerning cross-border environmental spillovers and there is actually a large number of agreements, for instance, on the abatement of chemicals which lead to acid rain or reductions in chlorofluorocarbons (CFCs). Co-operation has been achieved without recourse to trade sanctions. To base discussions on a firmer basis in this area, the Commission has launched an assessment of the effects of the EU's negotiating objectives for a new WTO round on sustainable development. A first report was issued in late 1999. The reports aim at maximising the benefits of liberalisation, while minimising potential negative side-effects. While the case for co-operation on cross-border pollution is well established, it is difficult to come up with a strong economic case for changing standards in other countries, where it comes to local pollution or social and human rights issues (Krugman, 1997). What matters for the gains from trade is that relative prices differ, be it for differences in resources, technologies, tastes, labour or environmental standards; and countries do have different ideas about what a reasonable standard is. In line with these arguments, the Community considers that differences in labour standards should not be used to justify protectionist measures and that comparative advantage of low-wage countries should not be put into question. On the other hand, it intends to promote core labour standards, such as the prohibition of slavery or the suppression of the exploitation of child labour and to find ways in multilateral fora, such as the WTO and the ILO, to do so. In addition, the GSP arrangements allow for the withdrawal of preferences to countries which countenance slavery and forced labour and since 1998 additional preferences have been granted to countries which respect the ILO conventions on the freedom of association, the right to collective bargaining and the Convention on child labour.

Notes

1. The single market programme was flanked by a strengthening in EU-wide competition policies, by a stepping up of inter-regional transfers and by providing for a few EU-wide competencies in the social area.
2. These restrictions were based on Article 115 (providing a safety valve for national governments to protect industries facing economic difficulties) and given practical effect through national control of internal frontiers.
3. Stevens and Young (1996) also provide an overview concerning changes for the other areas.
4. This number excludes quantitative restrictions covered by the derogations granted to Spain and Portugal upon their accession. The total number is 7 269 (Stevens and Young, 1996).
5. In 1988, roughly half of all textile and clothing imports into the European Union faced quantitative limitations, one-quarter was subject to the so-called "basket exit mechanism" but not restricted and about one quarter was not covered by any form of arrangement.
6. It is still legally possible to impose quantitative restrictions only in parts of the European Union but enforcement would be nearly impossible and no such measures have been taken since 1993.
7. In addition to the internal market legislation public procurement was liberalised in recent years by the European Economic Area Agreement, the revised WTO Agreement on Government Procurement, bilateral agreements and Association Agreements with the central and eastern European countries.
8. The United States Trade Representative annual review of EU obstacles to trade also points to areas in need of improvement. Similar exercises by the European Union concerning the United States ("United States Barriers to Trade and Investment") shows that the same is also true elsewhere.
9. WTO (1995) provides an overview of the development of regional agreements in a global context.
10. The convention provided for a considerable amount of aid in cash, duty-free access of industrial products and preferential treatment for competing (non-tropical) farm products. In return, the Associated States granted preferential treatment to imports from the common market.
11. The new European GSP scheme, which entered into force in 1995, comprises a general scheme and a special incentive scheme. The general scheme is based on a "tariff modulation mechanism", by which different preferential rates are applied to products according to their level of "sensitivity", and a "graduation mechanism" by which indices

of development and specialisation are used to determine whether GSP preferences apply to a specific country-product combination. Under the special incentive scheme, instead, supplementary preferential margins can be granted to countries that implement advanced social and environmental policies.

12. The tariff rates in Table 5 are estimates. While they probably give a good indication about trends, levels are subject to considerable uncertainty. Estimates by Curtis and Vastine (1971) for post-Kennedy Round tariff rates for industrial products give the following results:

	All items	Dutiable items only
United States	5.6	8.7
European Union	4.0	8.3
Japan	6.5	10.7
United Kingdom	8.0	10.9
Sweden	5.0	7.9
Denmark	3.8	7.9
Norway	4.1	10.2
Finland	6.8	11.2

Cline *et al.* (1978) estimate 1973 average tariff rates on all industrial imports of 4.2, 7.1 and 6.3 per cent for the EEC, the United States and Japan, respectively and of 9.0, 8.9 and 11.2 per cent respectively on dutiable imports.

13. While the principle of a Common Agricultural Policy was established with the Treaty of Rome, common policies were only introduced between 1962 and 1965 for the different agricultural products and common prices only between 1967 and 1968. Thorbecke and Pagoulatos (1975) provide an overview of the early development of the CAP.

14. The original GATT agreements, drafted during the 1940s, were intended to cover also agricultural products. As it worked out, however, agriculture had been largely excluded from the broad sweep of liberalisation. While agriculture also was prominent in the discussions of the Kennedy Round, results were minimal.

15. Tariff peaks will be lower than 15 per cent by the end of the implementation period, except for trucks and a few footwear items.

16. For instance in textile and clothing, leather, rubber, footwear and travel goods, fish and fish products, and transport equipment.

17. By the Uruguay Round Agreement on Agriculture, Members are committed to convert all non-tariff barriers into tariff equivalents (tariffication), followed by reductions on a simple average basis. In nearly all instances, the new tariffs consist of specific duties, for which the *ad valorem* equivalent cannot be easily calculated. Overall the tariffication requirement resulted in high levels of initial tariffs, due to both the high level of protection in the base period and to the level of prices used to calculate tariff equivalents.

18. In the European Union less than 12 per cent of tariff lines were duty free in 1996, as compared with about 18 per cent and 40 per cent respectively in the United States and Japan.

19. While 1996 *ad valorem* equivalents (AVEs) for specific and compound duties were available for the European Union and Canada, estimates from AVEs of base rates and bound rates are used for the other countries (OECD , 1997*a*).

20. The increase could also be partly explained by the different availability of estimates of *ad valorem* equivalents (AVEs) for specific duties in the two years. While the availability of estimates of AVEs for the United States and Japan has decreased from almost 100 per cent in 1988 and 1993 to 60 to 70 per cent in 1996, the availability of AVEs for the European Union has increased from less than 30 per cent in 1988 and 1993 to more than 80 per cent in 1996.
21. The dead-weight losses associated with a country's tariff structure depends not only on the average tariff rates and elasticities of demand and supply, but also on the variance in tariff rates across products.
22. The increase in the standard deviation can also be partly driven by the increase in the level of average protection, the mean of the sample over which the coefficient is calculated. In terms of welfare both the dispersion and the mean of the tariff structure are important. The relevant tariff in the case of the European Union is lower than the MFN applied rate due to the preferential agreements.
23. Tariff rates in excess of a given domestic reference level.
24. Declines in the tariff wedge as a result of trade liberalisation may lead to a decline in the effective rate of protection of the more processed product. This will depend on the elasticities of demand and supply, *i.e.* the net impact of tariff reductions on domestic demand and supply of final goods.
25. The import coverage ratio has the important drawback that those products facing very restrictive NTBs enter the calculation with a low weight.
26. The agreements reached in the Uruguay Round concern sanitary and phytosanitary measures, technical barriers to trade, anti-dumping, custom valuation, pre-shipment inspection, rules of origin, import licensing procedures, subsidies and countervailing measures and safeguards.
27. Existing grey area measures must be phased out within four years. The EU-Japan VER on automobiles was phased out in December 1999.
28. See for example Schott (1994) for a comprehensive assessment of the Uruguay Round agreements.
29. Since the conclusion of the Tokyo Round in 1979, the EC has undertaken some 550 anti-dumping investigations and less than twenty safeguard investigations (Bronckers, 1995). Explanations for the large difference in the use of the two instruments stems from the fact that anti-dumping measures can be requested directly by the industry, and that they can be adopted more easily than safeguards given the broader definition of dumping.
30. See Council Regulation 3283/94, as amended by Council Regulation 384/96.
31. Circumvention is defined as a change in trade patterns due to a practice, process or work for which there is insufficient due cause or economic justification, other than the imposition of the duty.
32. EU producers can complain that an anti-dumping measure has brought no or "insufficient" changes in resale or subsequent selling prices in the European Union and ask for an examination of the price effect. The Council may, by simple majority, amend the measure in force should the examination confirm "increased dumping" (WTO, 1996).
33. In line with the WTO Agreement, EU legislation incorporates a *de minimis* clause defining "negligible imports" to be excluded from an initiation. Countries representing a market share of less than 1 per cent of Community consumption of a product are excluded, unless the collective share of such countries amounts to 3 per cent or more as com-

pared with WTO limits of 3 and 7 per cent share of total imports respectively. It should be noted that the Community legislation uses a consumption benchmark to set the *de minimis* import levels rather than the volume of imports as specified in the WTO agreement.

34. Commission's 11th Report on the Community's Anti-dumping and Anti-subsidy Activities (1993).

35. These conditions stipulate that the parts imported from the targeted country amount to at least 60 per cent of the total value of the parts incorporated in the final product, and that the value added to the imported parts during assembly within the European Union does not exceed 25 per cent of the manufacturing cost.

36. See Messerlin (1991) or Vermulst (1987).

37. The rise in the Producer Support Estimate as a per cent of production is also affected by the 17 per cent decline in agricultural value added between 1997 and 1999.

38. ACP bananas continued to enter the Community duty-free but dollar fruit was to be subject to a two-tier tariff. A tariff of ECU 100 per tonne was set on the first two million tonnes of imports from Latin America; for imports above this threshold, the duty increased to ECU 850 per tonne. In 1992, this corresponded to a lower 24 per cent *ad valorem* tariff and to a higher 206 per cent tariff above the quota threshold.

39. He calculates a "Revealed Relative Restrictiveness" Index. The underlying assumption is that the more liberal a country, the less constrained its government can be expected to be in binding the *status quo* in the GATS. Hence the higher the coverage ratio of its schedule, the more liberal the country is relative to other countries.

40. Commitments can be broken down into three broad categories: "None", implying no restrictions are applied on either market access or national treatment for a given mode of supply/sector; "Unbound", meaning no commitment is made for a given mode of supply/sector; and "Other" which, in practice, implies that bound restrictions are listed for a mode of supply/sector. The weights used to calculate coverage ratios are obtained as follows: a value of "1" is allocated to all instances where "None" is found; a zero in all instances of "Unbound"; and 0.5 if specific bound restrictions are listed. The resulting ratios range from 0 (no restrictions) to 1 (no access). To estimate a country specific "tariff equivalent", each average coverage ratio is multiplied by a benchmark "guesstimate" of what the tariff equivalent of the most protectionist nation might be. The "tariff equivalent" list for the most restrictive country is completely arbitrary. A value of 200 was chosen for sectors where access tends to be prohibited by most countries, and which do not appear in most schedules (maritime cabotage, air transport except for ground services, postal services, voice telecommunications, and life insurance). The rest varies between 20 and 50 per cent.

41. They abolished national exclusivity rights and granted full cabotage rights. The single market in air transport services was completed with the full implementation of the liberalisation packages in April 1997.

42. This enables someone receiving data over electronic networks to determine the origin of the data and to check that data have not been altered.

43. Examples of information society services are on-line newspapers, on-line databases, on-line financial services, on-line professional services, on-line entertainment services such as video on demand, on-line direct marketing and advertising and services providing access to the World Wide Web.

44. The European Union suggested the following issues to be included in the WTO work programme on electronic commerce: legal treatment of electronic transactions especially in relation to the GATS agreement, custom duties on electronic transactions, privacy (in relation to Article XVI of the GATS), competition (with reference to Article IX of the GATS), intellectual property, trade facilitation, government procurement, information technology and standards. See 2nd Communication by the European Union and its Member States, *http://europa.eu.int/comm/trade/services/ecommerce/ecom3.htm*.
45. To enjoy the benefits of this "safe harbor", companies must bind themselves publicly to the "safe harbor" principles. Compliance will be checked in the first instance by private sector bodies, but non-compliance will also be subject to legal sanctions, notably under Section 5 of the US Federal Trade Commission Act, which forbids misrepresentation and deceptive trade practices (*e.g.* announcing adherence to a privacy arrangement and then ignoring it). The approval of this arrangement by the European Union will involve the Commission, EU Member States and the European Parliament. See *http://europa.eu.int/comm/internal_market/en/media/dataprot/index.htm* .
46. TBTs can take the form of technical regulations imposed by national governments, mainly for health, safety and environmental protection for the consumers; and non-regulatory barriers imposed by groups, trade associations, institutions, etc. Such barriers require either the application of technical specifications or standards to products, or the testing and certification of products or suppliers. TBTs impose additional costs on importers that are not faced by domestic suppliers. The magnitude of these costs may vary and can make imported products not competitive or unacceptable in the target market. Delays are often caused by conformity testing which can create an effective barrier to entry.
47. Under a MRA, each party is given the authority to test and certify products against the regulatory requirement of the other party, in its own territory and prior to export. MRAs do not require prior harmonisation of each party's requirements, so that each country's "technical culture" is preserved (Clarke, 1996).
48. The literature on the impact of standardisation on international trade is still very incomplete; see Matutes and Regibeau (1996) for a review. Another line of research which is relevant to market access issues is the one on the use of standardisation policies for entry deterrence.
49. Anderson and Norheim (1993) analyse trade integration globally since the 1830s. They find that the propensity to trade extra-regionally increased throughout the hundred years to 1928, that it fell in the 1930s and then increased for virtually all regions (though least so for Europe) since then. The slower increase for Europe is largely explained by the switch from colonial trade of Britain and France towards intra-European trade.
50. Analysis of the trade effects of the customs union between the original six members of the EEC (Balassa, 1975*a*) indicated that trade creation outweighed trade diversion for manufactured products until the early seventies, while the opposite was true for agricultural products, with the balance between the two being difficult to establish.
51. Bayoumi and Eichengreen also review earlier studies using gravity models.
52. For a review see Blomström and Kokko (1997).
53. Except for some service sectors where barriers to trade and investment before the single market programme were particularly high (*e.g.* in finance, insurance and telecommunication) (Dunning, 1997).
54. Empirical estimates of European integration in the 1960s using this approach showed that gains due to tariff reductions might have been very small (Balassa, 1975*a*). Indeed,

given the large share of two-way trade and similarity in factor endowments only small gains from exploiting comparative advantage could be expected.

55. Annex VI of OECD (2000*c*) provides an overview of the recent literature on market segmentation.

56. See the European Commission's extensive work on this.

57. Coe and Moghadam's results point to fairly strong gains from integration, the integration variable contributing ¾ per cent annually to growth between 1971 and 1986 and still ¼ per cent annually between 1987 and 1991.

58. According to Italianer's (1994) estimates, intra-EU integration has contributed nearly 0.3 percentage point to output growth per year over the whole sample period 1961-92. The impact of openness over the same period would instead be an average of 0.2 percentage point per year. Estimations for the different sub-periods show a very strong EU6 integration effect compared to openness for the period 1961-73. For the period 1974-86, EU6 integration has had a negative impact on growth and no impact if EU12 integration is considered. In 1987-92, intra-EU6 integration did not contribute to growth while intra-EU12 has by 0.4 per cent per year.

59. The Stolper-Samuelson theorem underlines the linkage between relative output prices and relative wages. Trade liberalisation between skilled-labour-abundant OECD countries and unskilled-labour-abundant countries will lead to a decline in the relative price of unskilled-labour-intensive products imported from low-wage countries. This in turn will lead to a more than proportionate cut in the relative wage of unskilled labour.

60. Integration, by preventing price segmentation raises perceived demand elasticities and leads to a reduction in the producer's average mark-up. This induces market exit of non-profitable firms, while the remaining producers can fully exploit economies of scale.

61. Hoekman (1996*b*) reviews additional proposals and the relevance for WTO negotiations.

62. "Community external trade policy in the field of standards and conformity assessment". Communication of the Commission: COM(96)564 final, 13 November 1996.

63. Annual Report of the President of the United States on the Trade Agreements Program (1996).

64. Of the 69 WTO working parties considering regional agreements only six were able to reach agreement on the compatibility with Article XXIV.

65. They were three in total and all concerned the European Union.

66. Free trade would conflict with the Common Agricultural Policy where it provides for limits on production, high levels of external protection and high support prices (see above).

67. As the EAs required the time-consuming process of ratification by all EU parliaments and the parliament of the respective CEEC, IAs have been concluded as an intermediate solution in each of the CEECs providing a legal framework for trade co-operation.

68. These new agreements are intended to replace the Co-operation Agreements currently in force between the European Union and its Mediterranean partners dating from the 1970s.

69. Local content requirements are often 60 per cent, *i.e.* to benefit from duty-free access to the European Union, 60 per cent of the value added must originate in either the European Union or in the partner country.

70. This act allows US citizens to sue in US courts any foreign company or individual deemed to have benefited from investments in property confiscated by the Cuban government following the Cuban revolution in 1959. Title IV of the Act also imposes visa restrictions on individuals with links to companies suspected of investing in such property.

Glossary of acronyms and terms

Acronyms

ACP	African, Caribbean and Pacific
AD	Anti-dumping
AMA	Anti-monopoly act
AVE	*Ad valorem* equivalent
CAB	Conformity Assessment Body
CAP	Common Agricultural Policy
CEFTA	Central European Free Trade Agreement
CEECs	Central and East European Countries
CGE	Computable general equilibrium
CVM	Countervailing measures
EA	Europe Agreement
EC	European Community
EEA	European Economic Area
EEC	European Economic Community
ECU	European currency unit
EFTA	European Free Trade Association
EMAs	Euro-Mediterranean Association Agreements
EU	European Union
FDI	Foreign Direct Investment
GATS	General Agreement on Trade in Services
GATT	General Agreement on Tariffs and Trade
GDP	Gross Domestic Product
GMO	Genetically Modified Organism
GNP	Gross National Product
GSP	Generalised System of Preferences
IA	Interim Agreement
ISIC	International Standard Industrial Classification
ITA	Information and Technology Agreement
IMF	International Monetary Fund
LDC	Least Developed Countries
MERCOSUR	Southern Common Market
MFA	Multifiber Arrangement
MFN	Most Favoured Nation
MNE	Multinational enterprise
MRA	Mutual Recognition Agreement
NACE	Statistical Classification of Economic Activities in the European Community
NAFTA	North American Free Trade Agreement

NGO	Non-governmental Organisation
NIS	Newly Independent States
NTA	New Transatlantic Agenda
NTB	Non-tariff Barrier
PCA	Partnership and Co-operation Agreement
PCM	Price Control Measure
PPP	Purchasing Power Parity
QR	Quantitative Restriction
Quad	GATT/WTO group of four: Canada, European Union, Japan and United States
R&D	Research and Development
SMPS	Single Market Program in Services
TBT	Technical Barrier to Trade
TPR	Trade Policy Review
TRIPs	Trade Related aspects of Intellectual Property Rights
URAA	Uruguay Round Agreement on Agriculture
USITC	United States International Trade Commission
VEPR	Voluntary Export Price Restraint
VER	Voluntary Export Restraint
WTO	World Trade Organisation

Terms

Anti-dumping measures

Measures that can be adopted after an investigation, by the investigating authority of the importing country, when dumping and material injury resulting therefrom has occurred. Dumping takes place when a product is exported at less than its normal value, *i.e.* the comparable price, in the ordinary course of trade, for the like product when consumed in the exporting country. Anti-dumping measures may take the form of anti-dumping duties or of price undertakings. Anti-dumping duties are generally enterprise-specific duties levied on certain goods to offset the dumping margin. Anti-dumping price undertakings may be offered to exporters to avoid the imposition of anti-dumping duties.

Binding

Commitment under GATT or GATS to keep the market open or (in the case of GATS) to provide national treatment, specifying maximum level of trade barriers. It requires negotiations and possibly compensation if a trade barrier is to be raised beyond the bound ceiling.

Countervailing measures

Measures that can be taken whenever an investigation, by the investigating authority of the importing country, has led to the determination that the imported goods are benefiting from subsidies, and that they result in an injury. Countervailing measures may take the form of countervailing duties or of undertakings by the exporting firms or by the authorities of the subsidising country.

Export restraints arrangement

Agreements by which an exporter agrees to limit exports in order to avoid imposition of mandatory restrictions by the importing country. The arrangement may be concluded either at the industry or government level. These arrangements are known as voluntary export restraints arrangements (VERs) and in the latter case as orderly marketing arrangements, etc. In addition to bilateral agreements there is also the Multilateral Multifibre Arrangement (MFA) which regulates trade in textile products. The MFA provides the framework and rules for negotiating bilateral restraint agreements. An MFA quota agreement establishes an export quota with a growth rate.

Most Favoured Nation (MFN)

Treatment: principle of non discrimination embodied in Article I of the General Agreement on Tariffs and Trade (GATT), whereby any concession or privilege granted by one contracting party to GATT to a product of another contracting party will be unconditionally granted to the like product of all other contracting parties. In practice, the MFN treatment is no longer limited to GATT contracting parties but applicable to other trading partners.

National Treatment

Principle of non discrimination between a country's own nationals and foreigners, embodied in Article 17 of the GATS.

Non-automatic licensing

The practice to require, as a prior condition to import, an import licence which is not granted automatically. The licence may either be issued on a discretionary basis or may depend on specific criteria.

Preferential duties under trade agreements

Duties applicable under multilateral or bilateral trade agreements or duties extended without reciprocity by one group of countries to another group of countries (*e.g.* the Generalized System of Preferences, GSP). These duties may be applied with no limitation of quantity or may be linked to preferential tariff quotas.

Variable charges

Charges that bring the market prices of imported agricultural and food products close to those of corresponding domestic products, in advance, for a given period of time, and for a pre-established price. These prices are known as reference prices, threshold or trigger prices. Primary commodities may be charged per total weight, while charges on processed foodstuff can be levied in proportion to the primary products contents in the final product. In the case of the European Union, the charges applied to primary products as such are called variable levies and those as part of a processed product, variable components.

Voluntary export price restraint

A restraint arrangement in which the exporter agrees to keep the price of his goods above a certain level.

Bibliography

Agarwal, J. P., U. Hiemenz and P. Nunnenkamp (1995),
"European Integration: A Threat to Foreign Investment in Developing Countries", *Kiel Institute Discussion Paper* No. 246, Kiel Institut für Weltwirtschaft an der Universität Kiel.

Ahn, S. and P. Hemmings (2000),
"Policy Influences on Economic Growth in OECD Countries: An Evaluation of the Evidence", OECD *Economics Department Working Papers*, No. 246.

Alonso-Gamo, P., S. Fennell and K. Sakr (1997),
"Adjusting to New Realities: MENA, the Uruguay Round and the EU-Mediterranean Initiative", IMF *Working Paper*, January.

Anderson, K. and H. Norheim (1993),
History, Geography and Regional Economic Integration, Regional Integration and the Global Trading System, K. Anderson and R. Blackhurst (eds.), Harvester Wheatsheaf.

Atkins, W. S. (1996),
"Technical Barriers to Trade", *The EU Single Market Review Series*, European Commission, November.

Backus D., T. Kehoe and P. Kehoe (1992),
"In search of Scale Effects and in Trade and Growth", *Journal of Economic Theory*, No. 58(2), December.

Balassa, B. (1975*a*),
"Trade Creation and Trade Diversion in the European Common Market: An Appraisal of the Evidence", in Balassa (ed.), *European Economic Integration*, Amsterdam.

Balassa, B. (1975*b*),
European Economic Integration, Contributions to Economic Analysis 89, Amsterdam.

Baldwin, R. E. and E. Seghezza (1996*a*),
"Growth and European Integration: Towards an Empirical Assessment", CEPR *Discussion Paper*, No. 1393.

Baldwin, R. E. and E. Seghezza (1996*b*),
"Testing for Trade-Induced Investment-Led Growth", CEPR *Discussion Paper*, No. 1331.

Barro, R. J. (1991),
"Economic Growth in a Cross Section of Countries", *Quarterly Journal of Economics*, 106(2).

Bayoumi, T. and B. Eichengreen (1995),
"Is Regionalism Simply a Diversion? Evidence from the Evolution of the EC and EFTA", IMF *Working Paper*, WP/95/109.

Bhagwati, J. and A. Panagariya (1996),
"The Theory of Preferential Trade Agreements: Historical Evolution and Current Trends", *American Economic Review*, Papers and Proceedings, May.

Blomstrom, M. and A. Kokko (1997),
"Regional Integration and Foreign Direct Investment", CEPR *Discussion Paper Series*, No. 1659, June.

Bourgeois, J. H. J. (1994),
"L'avis de la Cour de justice des Communautés européennes à propos de l'Uruguay Round: un avis mitigé", *Revue du Marché Unique Européen*, No. 4.

Bronckers , M. C. E. J. (1995),
"WTO Implementation in the European Community. Anti-dumping, Safeguards and Intellectual Property", *Journal of World Trade*, Vol. 29, No. 5, October.

Brown, D. K., A. V. Deardorff, A. K. Fox and R. M. Stern (1995),
"Computational Analysis of Goods and Services Liberalization in the Uruguay Round", The Uruguay Round and the Developing Economies. *World Bank Discussion Paper*, No. 307.

Brown, D. K., A. V. Deardorff and R. M. Stern (1997),
"Some Economic Effects of the Free Trade Agreement Between Tunisia and the European Union", *Regional Partners in Global Markets: Limits and Possibilities of the Euro-Med Agreements*, CEPR.

Burda, M. and B. Dluhosch (1999),
"Globalisation and European Labour Markets", in H. Siebert (ed.), *Globalisation and Labour*, Institut für Weltwirtschaft an der Universität Kiel.

Burniaux, J-M. and J. Waelbroeck (1997),
"Has the Single Market Program Been Boosting European Growth?", mimeo.

CEPS (1996),
"The determinants of Foreign Direct Flows in Europe and the Impact of the Single Market", European Commission.

Clarke, J. (1996),
"Conformity Assessment – Mutual Recognition", in OECD (1996), *Consumer Safety Standards and Conformity Assessment*, Paris.

Cline, W. R., N. Kawanabe, T. O. M. Kronsjo and T. Williams (1978),
Trade Negotiations in the Tokyo Round. A Quantitative Assessment, Washington.

Coe, D. T. and E. Helpman (1995),
"International R&D Spillovers", *European Economic Review*, No. 39, 5.

Coe, D. T. and R. Moghadam (1993),
"Capital and Trade as Engines of Growth in France", IMF *Staff Papers*, Vol. 40, No. 3, September.

Coppel, J. (2000),
"E-Commerce: Impacts and Policy Challenges", OECD *Economics Department Working Papers*, No. 252.

Cortes, O. and S. Jean (1995),
"Commerce international et emploi : l'expérience européenne", *La Revue du* CEPII, No. 64.

Curtis, T. B. and J. R. Vastine (1971),
The Kennedy Round and the Future of American Trade, New York.

Dunning, J. H. (1997),
"The European Market Programme and Inbound Foreign Direct Investment", *Journal of Common Market Studies*, Vol. 35, No. 2, June.

Edwards, S. (1989),
"Openness, Outward Orientation, Trade Liberalization and Economic Performance in Developing Countries", NBER *Working Paper*, No. 2908, March.

Edwards, S. (1993),
"Openness, Trade Liberalization and Growth in Developing Countries", *Journal of Economic Literature*, No. XXXI.

Edwards, S. (1998),
"Openness, Productivity and Growth: What Do We Really Know?", NBER *Working Paper*, No. 5978, March.

Emiliou, N. (1996),
"The Death of Exclusive Competence?", *European Law Review*, Vol. 21.

European Commission (1988),
"The Economics of 1992", *European Economy*, No. 35.

European Commission (1993),
"The European Community as a World Trade Partner", *European Economy*, No. 52.

European Commission (1995*a*),
"Competition Policy in the New Trade Order: Strengthening International Co-operation and Rules", Report of the Group of Experts, mimeo, Brussels.

European Commission (1995*b*),
"Strengthening the Mediterranean Policy of the European Union: Establishing a Euro-Mediterranean Partnership", *Bulletin of the European Union*, Supplement 2/95.

European Commission (1996*a*),
The 1996 Single Market Review. Background Information for the Report to the Council and the European Parliament, SEC(96)2378, Brussels.

European Commission (1996*b*),
"Economic Evaluation of the Internal Market", *European Economy Reports and Studies*, No. 4.

European Commission (1996*c*),
WTO Aspects of EU Preferential Trade Agreements with Third Countries.

European Commission (1996*d*),
The Global Challenge of International Trade: A *Market Access Strategy for the European Union*, COM(96)53 final, 14 February.

European Commission (1997*a*),
"The European Union as a World Trade Partner", *European Economy, Reports and Studies*, No. 3.

European Commission (1997*b*),
"Agenda 2000; For a Stronger and Wider Union", *Bulletin of the European Union*, Supplement 5/97.

European Commission (1999),
Enlargement Commission Reports 1999, *Second Report for each of the candidates countries of Central and Eastern Europe*, October.

EUROSTRATEGY (1996),
"Single Market Review 1996. Dismantling of Barriers: Public procurement", mimeo.

Fernández, R. and J. Portes (1998),
"Returns to Regionalism: An Analysis of Non-traditional Gains from Regional Agreements", *The World Bank Economic Review*, Vol. 12, No. 2.

Fontagné, L., M. Freudenberg and D. Ünal-Kezenci (1996),
"Les Échanges de Biens Intermédiaires de la Triade", *Économie Internationale*, 65.

Fontagné, L. and M. Freudenberg (1997),
"Intra-industry Trade: Methodological Issues Reconsidered", CEPII Document de Travail No. 97-01, January.

François, J. F., B. McDonald and H. Nordström (1996),
"Assessing the Uruguay Round", The Uruguay Round and the Developing Economies, *World Bank Discussion Paper*, No. 307.

Frankel, J. A., E. Stein and S-J. Wei (1996),
"Regional Trading Arrangements: Natural or Supernatural", *American Economic Review*, Papers and Proceedings, May.

Frankel, J. A. and D. Romer (1999),
"Does Trade Cause Growth?", *American Economic Review*, No. 89.

Freeman, R. B. and A. Revenga (1995),
"International Trade and Employment: the European Experience", paper presented at the ECARE/CEPII Workshop on International Trade and Employment, Palais du Luxembourg, Paris.

GATT (1980),
The Tokyo Round of Multilateral Negotiations, Vol. II, Geneva.

GATT (1994),
The Results of the Uruguay Round of Multilateral Trade Negotiations, Geneva, November.

Grether, J-M. and M. Olarreaga (1998),
"Preferential and Non-Preferential Trade Flows in World Trade", *Staff Working Paper* ERAD, No. 98-10, World Trade Organization.

Griliches, Z. and J. Mairesse (1995),
"Production Functions: the Search for Identification", NBER *Working Paper*, Series No. 5067, March.

Hathaway, D. E. and M. D. Ingco (1995),
"Agricultural Liberalisation and the Uruguay Round", *World Bank Discussion Papers*, No. 307.

Henrekson, M., J. Torstensson and R. Torstensson (1997),
"Growth Effects of European Integration", *European Economic Review*, Vol. 41, No. 8.

Hoekman, B. (1995),
"Assessing the General Agreement on Trade in Services", *World Bank Discussion Papers*, No. 309.

Hoekman, B. (1996*a*),
"Multilateral Disciplines on Government Procurement: What's in it for Developing Countries?" CEPR *Discussion Paper*, No. 1502, October.

Hoekman, B. (1996*b*),
"Trade and Competition Policy in the WTO System", CEPR *Discussion Paper* Series, No. 1501.

Hoekman, B. and S. Djankov (1995),
"The European Union's Mediterranean Free Trade Initiative", *The World Economy*, Vol. 19.

Hoeller, P., N. Girouard and A. Colecchia (1998),
"The European Union's Trade Policies and Their Economic Effects", OECD *Economics Department Working Papers*, No. 194.

Italianer, A. (1994),
"Whither the Gains from European Economic Integration", *Revue Économique*, Vol. 45, No. 3, May.

Jaquemin, A. and A. Sapir (1988),
"European Integration or World Integration?", *Weltwirtschaftliches Archiv*, No. 124.

Krugman, P. (1991),
"Is Bilateralism Bad?", in E. Helpman and A. Razin (eds), *International Trade and Trade Policy*, Cambridge.

Krugman, P. (1997),
"What Should Trade Negotiators Negotiate About?" *Journal of Economic Literature*, Vol. XXXV, No. 1, March.

Lamy, P. (2000),
"What are the Options after Seattle", Speech to the European Parliament, 25 January.

Lawrence, R. Z. (1996),
Regionalism, Multilateralism, and Deeper Integration, The Brookings Institution, Washington.

Lee, J. W. (1993),
"International Trade, Distortions and Long Run Growth", IMF *Staff Papers*, No. 40, 2.

Lee, J. W. (1994),
"Capital Goods Imports and Long Run Growth", NBER *Working Paper*, No. 4725.

Levine, R. and D. Renelt (1991),
"Cross-Country Studies of Growth and Policy. Methodological, Conceptual and Statistical Problems", *World Bank Working Papers Series*, No. 608, March.

Levine, R. and D. Renelt (1992),
"A Sensitivity Analysis of Cross-Country Growth Regressions", *American Economic Review* 82, No. 4.

Marks G., L. Hooghe and K. Blank (1996),
"European Integration from the 1980s: State-Centric v. Multi-level Governance", *Journal of Common Market Studies*, Vol. 34, No. 3, September.

Matusz, S. J. and D. G. Tarr (1999),
"Adjusting to Trade Policy Reform", *Policy Research Working Paper*, No. 2142, World Bank.

Matutes, C. and P. Regibeau (1996),
"A selective Review of the Economics of Standardisation. Entry, Deterrence, Technologial Progress and International Competition", *European Journal of Political Economy*, Vol. 12.

Mercenier, J. (1995),
"Can '1992' Reduce Unemployment in Europe? On Welfare and Employment Effects of Europe's Move to a Single Market", *Journal of Policy Modeling* 17, February.

Messerlin, P. A. (1991),
"The Uruguay Negotiations on Anti-dumping Enforcement: Some Basic Issues", *Policy Implications of Anti-dumping Measures*, North-Holland, Amsterdam.

Messerlin, P. A. (1993),
"Services in the European Economy as a World Trade Pattern," *European Economy*, No. 52.

Messerlin, P. A. (1996),
"The Re-emergence of Trade among the East European and Baltic Countries: Commercial and other Policy Issues", *Economic Bulletin for Europe*, Vol. 48.

Messerlin, P. A. (1999),
Measuring the Costs of Protection in Europe, Institute for International Economics, Washington, D.C.

Nagarajan, N. (1999),
"The Millennium Round: An Economic Appraisal", ECFIN *Economic Papers*, No. 139.

Neven, D. and L. H. Roeller (1991),
"European Integration and Trade Flows", *European Economic Review*, Vol. 35, No. 6.

Neven, D. and C. Wyplosz (1996),
"Relative Prices, Trade and Restructuring in European Industry", CEPR *Discussion Paper*, No. 1451, August.

Nicoletti, G., S. Scarpetta and O. Boylaud (1999),
"Summary Indicators of Product Market Regulation with an Extension to Employment Protection Legislation", OECD *Economics Department Working Papers*, No. 226.

OECD (1995),
The Uruguay Round: A Preliminary Evaluation of the Impacts of the Agreement on Agriculture in the OECD *countries*, Paris.

OECD (1996),
Agricultural Policies, Markets and Trade in OECD *Countries*, Paris.

OECD (1997*a*),
Indicators of Tariff and Non-tariff Trade Barriers, Paris.

OECD (1997*b*),
The Uruguay Round Agreement on Agriculture and Processed Agricultural Products, Paris.

OECD (1997*c*),
"Recent Trends in Foreign Direct Investment", *Financial Market Trends*, No. 67.

OECD (1997*d*),
Employment Outlook, July.

OECD (1998),
Open Markets Matter: The Benefits of Trade and Investment Liberalisation, Paris.

OECD (2000*a*),
"Local Access Pricing and E-Commerce", Paris.

OECD (2000*b*),
Agricultural Policies in OECD *Countries. Monitoring and Evaluation* 2000, Paris.

OECD (2000*c*),
EMU. *One Year On*, Paris.

Presa, S. (1993),
"A Concise Overview of the EC Trade Policy", *European Economy*, No. 52.

Resnick, S. A. and E. M. Truman (1975),
"An Empirical Examination of Bilateral Trade in Western Europe", *European Economic Integration*.

Rodríguez, R. and D. Rodrik (1999),
"Trade Policy and Economic Growth: A Sceptic's Guide to the Cross-national Evidence", mimeo. Available at: *http://www.ksg.harvard.edu/rodrik/skepti1299.pdf*.

Romer, P. M. (1987),
"Growth based on increasing returns due to specialisation", *American Economic Review*, Vol. 77, No. 2, May.

Rutherford, T., E. Rutström and D. Tarr (1995),
"The Free Trade Agreement Between Tunisia and the European Union", World Bank, mimeo.

Sapir, A. (1998),
"The Political Economy of EC Regionalism", *European Economic Review*, Vol. 42, No. 3-5.

Schiff, M. and A. Winters (1998),
"Regional Integration as Diplomacy", *The World Bank Economic Review*, Vol. 12, No. 2.

Schott, J. J. (1994),
The Uruguay Round. An Assessment, Institute for International Economics, Washington, November.

Slaughter, M. J. (1998),
"International Trade and Labour-Market Outcomes: Results, Questions, and Policy Options", *The Economic Journal*, Vol. 108, No. 450.

Stevens, C. and A. Young (1996),
"Single Market Review 1996. Impact of Trade and Investment. External Access to European Markets: Legal and Descriptive Analysis", Institute of Development Studies, November.

Sykes, A. O. (1995),
"Product Standards for Internationally Integrated Goods Markets", The Brookings Institution, Washington D.C.

Thorbecke, E. and E. Pagoulatos (1975),
"The Effects of European Economic Integration on Agriculture", in Balassa (ed.), *European Economic Integration*.

Vamvadakis, A. (1998),
"Regional Integration and Economic Growth", *The World Bank Review*, Vol. 12, No. 2.

Vermulst, E. A. (1987),
Anti-dumping law and practice in the United States and the European Communities, North-Holland, Amsterdam.

Vona, S. (1991),
"On the Measurement of Intra-industry Trade: Some Further Thoughts", *Weltwirtschaftliches Archiv*, 127(4).

Wallace, H. and W. Wallace (ed.) (1996),
Policy-making in the European Union, Oxford University Press.

Winters, A. (1996),
"Regionalism versus Multilateralism", CEPR *Discussion Paper*, No. 1525, November.

Witherell, W. H. (1996),
"Towards an International Set of Rules for Investment", Towards Multilateral Investment Rules, OECD *Documents*.

Wood, A. (1998),
"Globalisation and Labour Market Adjustment", *The Economic Journal*, Vol. 108, No. 450.

WTO (1995),
Regionalism and the World Trading System, Geneva.

WTO (1996),
Trade Policy Review, European Union, Geneva.

WTO (2000*a*),
Trade Policy Review, European Union, Geneva.

WTO (2000*b*),
Annual Report 2000, Geneva.

Yeats, A. (1997),
"Does Mercosur's Trade Performance Raise Concerns about the Effects of Regional Trade Arrangements?", *World Bank Policy Research Working Paper*, No. 1729.

Annex I

The institutional framework and treaty provisions

The institutional framework

Trade policy in the European Union is by-and-large correctly perceived to be essentially a competence of the Community. But matters are never quite so simple, and a number of considerations need to be taken into account in assessing the functioning of the institutional framework. Policy making in the European Union is characterised by mutual dependence, complementary functions and overlapping competencies between different bodies. The Single European Act and the Maastricht Treaty, by establishing co-operation and co-decision procedures, have transformed the legislative process from a Council-dominated process to a complex interplay between Council, Parliament and Commission. These procedures give the Commission a significant agenda-setting capacity and make it a sort of broker between the two institutions.[1] Overall, the Commission is a crucial actor in the policy initiation phase; it has substantial executive autonomy in the areas of agriculture, trade and competition and contributes to decision-making in other areas by influence rather than sanction. Also the Court of Justice, which ensures the interpretation and the application of the treaties, is playing an increasingly important role in this mutually dependent decision-making process.

Community law is anchored in the Treaties and includes a common commercial policy[2] whose purpose is the following:

> By establishing a customs union between themselves Member States aim to contribute, in the common interest, to the harmonious development of world trade, the progressive abolition of restrictions on international trade and the lowering of customs barriers. The common commercial policy shall take into account the favourable effect, which the abolition of customs duties between Member States may have on the increase in the competitive strength of undertakings in those States (Treaty of Rome, 1957).

The sections of the EC Treaty concerning the common commercial policy underwent only minor modifications under the Maastricht and Amsterdam Treaties. The Treaty provisions concerning trade policies (Articles 110-116) are reproduced below. In addition, the Council can also take trade policy measures, if this is needed to attain the overall objectives of the Community and the Treaty does not provide explicitly for the necessary powers (Article 235).

Qualified majority voting in the Council has now been extended to most of the policy areas covered by the original Treaty of Rome, including agriculture, competition policy, transport, and policy areas concerned with the implementation of the single market.[3] Decision-making concerning trade in goods is also governed by qualified majority voting except for initiatives under Article 235. This has contributed to a more rapid and effective decision-making process in this field. In addition, consultations with the Parliament are usually not obligatory, even though a regular information process has in recent years been initiated by the Commission. A Council decision is required for the Commission to enter into negotiations with third countries, usually on the basis of a negotiating directive. A Committee consisting of national high-level trade officials – the so-called Article 133 Committee – co-ordinates the negotiations and gives advice to the Commission as negotiator. It aims at ensuring that agreements with third countries will not run into strong opposition by Member States and will be approved by the Council upon completion of the negotiations.

The common commercial policy falls under the exclusive competence of the Community and covers trade in goods, including agriculture, nuclear products as covered by Euratom, as well as coal and steel products as covered by the European Coal and Steel Community. Competencies in other trade areas are split between the Community and Member States, but 1971 and 1976 Court of Justice rulings made it clear that the Community has external competence also in the fields in which it has internal competence,[4] because bilateral international treaties could lead to an uneven internal playing field.

Nonetheless, the Community's exclusive competence in the field of commercial policy has continued to arouse controversy. Even on the occasion of the Uruguay Round there was disagreement between the Commission on the one hand, and the Council, the Member States and the European Parliament on the other, who should sign the agreement as the Member States took the view that the Final Act and the WTO Agreement covered matters of national competence (Emiliou, 1996). Hence, the WTO Agreement was signed by representatives of both the EU Council and of the Member States on behalf of their respective governments. Who controls a negotiating mandate is also controversial. The Commission negotiates on the basis of a mandate that has been agreed by the Council, but there is plenty of scope for different interpretations of the mandate. At the WTO Ministerial Conference in Seattle in 1999, for instance, the Commission agreed to the establishment of a WTO Working Group on Biotechnology only to find itself rebuked by Member States who repudiated the tentative deal.

In contrast to trade in goods, the Community never had a clear mandate to negotiate and implement trade policies in the services sector. Therefore the Court of Justice was asked to provide a ruling on the matter. The 1994 Court ruling concluded that the Community had exclusive jurisdiction to conclude the Multilateral Agreement on Trade in Goods and that also trade in services could not in principle be excluded from the Community's competence.[5] As concerns the General Agreement on Trade in Services (GATS), the Court ruled that it should fall under the scope of the EU's external competence under Article 133 (formerly Article 113). That implies, however, that areas already covered by other policies set out in the EC Treaty, such as those concerning most modes of services supply[6] and transport policy, as well as other issues covered by GATS but not dealt with by Treaty provisions at all, remain within the competence of Member States. As concerns the Agreement on Trade-related Aspects of Intellectual Property Rights (TRIPS), only border measures fall under the competence of the Community. Since the ratification of the 1997 Amsterdam Treaty, the Article 133 powers have been extended to negotiations and agreements on services and intellectual property rights. However, unanimity is required in the Council's voting.

The decision-making power was delegated from the Council to the Commission in some areas, for instance, in anti-dumping cases and safeguard actions. Nevertheless, the rules often provide for the possibility of further review by the Council, which can confirm, reject, or modify the Commission's decision. A few other trade-related areas fall under partial competence of the Community, especially to ensure that uniform conditions prevail in the internal market. That is the case of competition policy (including subsidies), public procurement and export promotion.

While decision-making on issues related to trade in goods is less cumbersome than in many other areas of Community policy, policy decisions are still the outcome of intensive bargaining and negotiation processes. Concerning the Commission's work, difficulties and divided situations may appear at different levels of the decision process. For instance, there can be disagreement within the Commission on the analysis of facts and the appropriate measures to be taken. Another layer of complexity is due to the need to reach a compromise among 15 Member States, the bargaining behaviour of which is dictated by domestic preferences and general trade philosophy that still diverges considerably across countries.[7]

Concerning trade in services and other trade-related issues, decision-making is even more complex due to the restrictive interpretation of Article 133 by the Court of Justice. This is of particular concern, given the number of new trade issues emerging on the agenda of the WTO. The current set-up could make future negotiations cumbersome, as the outcome of negotiations is usually presented as a "single undertaking". This implies that, if part of the negotiated agenda is not under the sole competence of the Council, unanimity is required for the entire agenda, even though part of the overall "undertaking" could concern goods.

Commercial policy and provisions[8]

Article 110

By establishing a customs union between themselves Member States aim to contribute, in the common interest, to the harmonious development of world trade, the progressive abolition of restrictions on international trade and the lowering of customs barriers.

The common commercial policy shall take into account the favourable effect which the abolition of customs duties between Member States may have on the increase in the competitive strength of undertakings in those States.

Article 111

Article 111 has been repealed.[9]

Article 112

1. Without prejudice to obligations undertaken by them within the framework of other international organisations, Member States shall, progressively harmonize the systems whereby they grant aid for exports to third countries, to the extent necessary to ensure that competition between undertakings of the Community is not distorted.

On a proposal from the Commission, the Council, shall, acting by a qualified majority, issue any directives needed for this purpose.

2. The preceding provisions shall not apply to such drawback of customs duties or charges having equivalent effect nor to such repayment of indirect taxation including turnover taxes, excise duties and other indirect taxes as is allowed when goods are exported from a Member State to a third county, in so far as such drawback or repayment does not exceed the amount imposed, directly or indirectly, on the products exported.

Article 113

In 1992, Article 113 was replaced by the following:[9]

1. The common commercial policy shall be based on uniform principles, particularly in regard to changes in tariff rates, the conclusion of tariff and trade agreements, the achievement of uniformity in measures of liberalization, export policy and measures to protect trade such as those to be taken in the event of dumping or subsidies.

2. The Commission shall submit proposals to the Council for implementing the common commercial policy.

3. Where agreements with one or more States or international organisations need to be negotiated, the Commission shall make recommendations to the Council, which shall authorize the Commission to open the necessary negotiations.

The Commission shall conduct these negotiations in consultation with a special committee appointed by the Council to assist the Commission in this task and within the framework of such directives as the Council may issue to it.

The relevant provisions of Article 300 shall apply.

4. In exercising the powers conferred upon it by this Article, the Council shall act by a qualified majority.

New Article **113(5)** *of the* **TEC**

5. The Council, acting unanimously on a proposal from the Commission and after consulting the European Parliament, may extend the application of paragraphs 1 to 4 to international negotiations and agreements on services and intellectual property insofar as they are not covered by these paragraphs.

Article **114**

Article 114 has been repealed.[9]

Article **115**

In 1992, Article 115 was replaced by the following:[9]

In order to ensure that the execution of measures of commercial policy taken in accordance with this Treaty by any Member State is not obstructed by deflection of trade, or where differences between such measures lead to economic difficulties in one or more Member States, the Commission shall recommend the methods for the requisite cooperation between Member States. Failing this, the Commission may authorize Member States to take the necessary protective measures, the conditions and details of which it shall determine.

In case of urgency, Member States shall request authorization to take the necessary measures themselves from the Commission, which shall take a decision as soon as possible; the Member States concerned shall then notify the measures to the other Member States. The Commission may decide at any time that the Member States concerned shall amend or abolish the measures in question.

In the selection of such measures, priority shall be given to those which cause the least disturbance to the functioning of the common market.

Article **116**

Article 116 has been repealed.[9]

Article **235**

If action by the Community should prove necessary to attain, in the course of the operation of the common market, one of the objectives of the Community and this Treaty has not provided the necessary powers, the Council shall, acting unanimously on a proposal from the Commission and after consulting the European Parliament, take the appropriate measures.

Notes

1. Under the co-operation procedure, the Commission can set the agenda and may decide to take up or drop amendments from either the Council or the Parliament. According to the co-decision procedure, under which the Parliament has a veto power, if the Parliament or Council reject each other's position, a conciliation Committee is established. Such a Committee consists of representatives from both institutions, with the Commission acting as a broker. A compromise needs the approval of an absolute majority in the Parliament and of a qualified majority in the Council. If there is no agreement the initiative returns to the Council, which can make it a "take it or leave it" offer, which the Parliament can reject by absolute majority (Marks *et al.*, 1996).
2. Presa (1993) provides a concise overview of the common commercial policy and related legislation; and the WTO Trade Policy Reviews provide follow-ups on institutional changes.
3. There are some important exceptions which include the EU budget, taxation, capital flows, self-employed and professions, free movement of persons, and rights of employed persons (Marks *et al.*, 1996).
4. Competence is only established insofar as a common internal policy is effectively in place.
5. Bourgeois (1994) provides a legal interpretation of the Court ruling and an overview of its implications for international negotiations.
6. That is, in the case of commercial presence, consumption abroad and presence of persons.
7. Negotiation outcomes are often achieved through "side-payments" (*i.e.* compensation to a bargaining party that loses from a particular collective policy measure in order to gain political support from it); "log rolling" (*i.e.* a "vote trading" by which an actor votes for an issue that does not serve her/his interest in exchange for a positive vote on another issue); and "package deals" (*i.e.* issue-linkage, by which decisions are taken over different issue areas simultaneously to achieve support by all actors involved).
8. Treaty Establishing The European Economic Community, Rome, 25 March 1957.
9. Council of the European Communities, Commission of the European Communities (1992), Treaty on European Union, Luxembourg.

Annex II

Trade and growth in the European Union

In the following exercise, further evidence on the link between trade indicators and overall growth in the context of an aggregate production function approach is provided. A cross-country panel of eleven European countries is used to estimate a production function in annual growth rates over the period 1970-95.[1] The basic equation relates annual growth rates of GDP to growth rates in employment, capital stock and expenditure on research and development (R&D). An intra-industry trade index (S) is included in the production function estimates.[2] Following Italianer (1994) we also add to the regression a proxy for openness (O, defined as the share of total trade in GDP) and a proxy for European integration (I, defined as the share of area trade in total trade, by taking into account successive enlargements).[3] The introduction of these two trade indexes leads to an implicit test of whether regional trade has a stronger impact on productivity growth than trade in general. The exercise differs from that carried out by Italianer in at least three respects.

Firstly, growth in R&D expenditure is used here as a proxy for investment in human capital. Over the sample considered, the use of secondary enrolment rates or other education proxies does not seem to be appropriate to explain differences in productivity across European countries. Data on private R&D expenditure, on the contrary, mainly reflect expenditure on wages of researchers and scientists, and can be considered to be a proxy for investment in innovation activity.

Secondly, the analysis of the panel data reveals the presence of individual, time and joint effects. We test for the appropriate specification to be used in the estimation, which in all the three cases appears to be that of a fixed effects model rather than a random component model. The Fixed Effects (equation 16), the Feasible General Least Square estimators (equation 17) and the Hausman specification test are reported here for the case of individual effects. By allowing for country-specific intercepts, one can control for cross-country differences in total factor productivity growth or the residual of the estimated function. This specification implies a direct test of the impact of trade on total factor productivity, after having controlled for the impact of investment in human capital devoted to innovation, and for exogenous cross-country differences in technological progress.

Thirdly, the Grubel and Lloyd intra-industry trade index is introduced in the specification, in order to capture the productivity gains stemming from economies of scale and increased specialisation in production.[4] Obviously this index captures both intra-industry trade in intermediate inputs, from which positive externalities should be generated, and intra-industry trade in final consumption goods, which mainly produce welfare gains. Fontagné *et al.* (1996) estimate that the share of intra-industry trade consisting of intermediate inputs, carried out by the Community, is 36 per cent, while it is 38 per cent in the United States and 21 per cent in Japan. Moreover, 43 per cent of that share takes place within the

Community. The variable could therefore also capture the positive externalities associated with integration.

A production function in log terms (where lower cases are log variables) is estimated over a pooled dataset. This approach allows to exploit the time series as well as the cross section dimension of the data, where $i = 1$ to 11 is the country dimension and $t = 1970$ to 1995 is the time dimension. In first differences, real Gross Domestic Product (Y) is regressed on total employment (E), private sector capital stock (K) and private sector expenditure in research and development (R). Differencing equation A eliminates any fixed individual effects that might have been in the data. The resulting t-1 set of cross section of differences can be treated as a new pooled dataset.[5] The estimated base equations (3-6) are reported in Table A1. The analysis of variance on the residuals of the base equation points to the existence of individual, time and joint effects and varying variances across sections. The advantage of this transformation (differencing) is that it allows to take into account individual effects that change smoothly over time, but at different rates. In other words the presence of individual effects in the error term (or total factor productivity residual) allows to model productivity trends that differ across countries. The other advantage is that by expressing the production function in growth terms one can interpret the estimated coefficients in terms of elasticities.

$$\text{(A)} \qquad \Delta y_{it} = \beta_1 \Delta l_{it} + \beta_2 \Delta k_{it} + \beta_3 \Delta r_{it} + \Delta u_{it}$$

To control for the individual effects one should choose between fixed or random estimators. Given that the panel is composed of countries it is more likely that the best model is the dummy variable one. In this case, the inference is conditional on the individuals or cross-sectional units. Moreover if a correlation between the unmeasurable individual characteristics and the regressors exists, the random effects estimator will be biased, while the fixed effect estimator will not be. If one interprets the individual effects as cross country differences in the production function (a sort of TFP difference), then one might expect this correlation to exist.

Even if the fixed effect estimator is expected to be the best linear estimator, the Hausman specification test is calculated. Such a test is based on whether or not the difference between the estimators is significant. The within (fixed effects) estimator (equation 3) and the generalised least square (random effects) estimator (equation 17) are computed. If the null hypothesis is true, then, asymptotically, the two estimators differ only through sampling error. Rejection of the null hypothesis suggests that the error components model is not appropriate. The Hausman specification test gives a Chi-Squared (5) = 60.026 with significance level 0.000. Under the null hypothesis of no correlation between the regressors and the effects, the significance level below 0.5 or 0.1 indicates rejection of the null. It is better to use the fixed effects model.

Finally, to allow for individual heteroscedasticity of the disturbances, the variance in each cross-section is determined empirically and the fixed effect model is estimated by Weighted Least Squares (equation 18).

Changing the sample period reveals that these correlations are very sensitive (compare equations 7-10 and 11-15 in Table A1). In general the break is between the seventies-mid-eighties and the nineties. The sample is broken up into two sub-periods: 1970-82 and 1983-95, in order to have an approximately equal number of observations. In the fixed effect specialisation the coefficients of the intra-industry index and of R&D are left to vary across the two sample periods (see equation 2 in Table 14). While up to the early eighties the specialisation index seems to have played an important role, this effect disappears in the second period. On the other hand, the coefficient on R&D expenditure only becomes significant in the latter period. If R&D plays an increasingly important role in a cross-country aggregate production

Table A1. **Estimation by OLS**[3]

$$\Delta \ln Y = \alpha_0 + \alpha_1 \Delta \ln E + \alpha_2 \Delta \ln K + \alpha_3 \Delta O + \alpha_4 \Delta S + \alpha_5 \Delta I + \alpha_6 \Delta \ln R$$

	α_0	α_1	α_2	α_3	α_4	α_5	α_6	Rbar**2	DoF	DW
1970-95										
(3)	0.01	0.37	0.43					0.31	259	1.90
	(0.98)	(6.40)	(6.28)							
(4)	0.01	0.38	0.42	0.07				0.33	258	1.88
	(0.97)	(6.59)	(6.25)	(2.82)						
(5)	0.003	0.36	0.43	0.08	0.14			0.34	255	1.89
	(0.58)	(6.26)	(6.32)	(3.14)	(2.29)					
(6)	0.002	0.359	0.440	0.081	0.001	0.018		0.34	254	1.91
	(0.41)	(6.15)	(6.47)	(3.20)	(2.01)	(1.45)				
1970-82										
(7)	–0.02	0.32	0.76					0.27	119	2.13
	(1.85)	(2.04)	(5.67)							
(8)	–0.02	0.27	0.75	0.08				0.29	118	2.10
	(1.95)	(1.72)	(5.71)	(1.98)						
(9)	–0.02	0.24	0.72	0.09	0.18			0.30	117	2.13
	(1.90)	(1.56)	(5.47)	(2.25)	(2.03)					
(10)	–0.02	0.22	0.72	0.09	0.17	0.02		0.30	116	2.13
	(1.89)	(1.43)	(5.47)	(2.23)	(1.91)	(1.10)				
1983-95										
(11)	0.03	0.52	–0.15					0.44	127	1.73
	(4.21)	(7.87)	(0.93)							
(12)	0.02	0.48					0.05	0.52	123	1.76
	(5.20)	(10.19)					(2.67)			
(13)	0.02	0.49		0.07			0.05	0.54	122	1.75
	(5.02)	(10.60)		(2.57)			(2.93)			
(14)	0.02	0.50		0.07	0.00		0.05	0.54	116	1.73
	(4.76)	(10.11)		(2.48)	(0.00)		(2.69)			
(15)	0.02	0.50		0.07	0.00	0.01	0.05	0.54	115	1.77
	(4.70)	(10.15)		(2.60)	(0.00)	(1.05)	(2.60)			

3. **Variables:** Y = real GDP; E = total employment; K = private sector capital stock; R = private sector expenditure on Research and Development; O = share of total trade (imports + exports) in GDP; S = intra industry trade index; I = share of area trade in total trade which takes into account successive enlargements.
Sample: Yearly data (1970-95) for eleven EU countries (Luxembourg excluded). T-statistics in parenthesis. Country dummies are included. In equations 12 to 15, α_2 is not reported because it is not significant.

Source: OECD.

function, a further step could be the introduction of a proxy for trade as a vehicle of technology diffusion (as in Coe and Helpman, 1995).

In conclusion, an attempt is made to control for the channels through which trade could have an indirect impact on growth (physical capital formation, investment in R&D, country-specific differences in technical progress) and test whether, apart from the positive externalities generated by trade, additional gains to the eleven European countries could stem from increased trade on a multilateral or on a regional basis. The regressions show that the openness variable (O) has a significant and positive coefficient which is robust to changes in sample and estimation methods. The intra-industry trade index (S) is also positive over the whole sample period (equation 18) (Table A2). The coefficient, though, decreases dramati-

Table A2. **Estimation of individual effects**[1]

$\Delta \ln Y = \alpha_0 + \alpha_1 \Delta \ln E + \alpha_2 \Delta \ln K + \alpha_3 \Delta O + \alpha_4 \Delta S + \alpha_5 \Delta I$

	α_0	α_1	α_2	α_3	α_4	α_5	Rbar**2	DoF
(16) Fixed Effects Estimator		0.36 (6.18)	0.44 (6.46)	0.081 (3.19)	0.001 (2.00)	0.018 (1.45)	0.33	254
(17) Feasible General Least Square Estimator	0.010 (4.18)	0.38 (6.61)	0.35 (6.10)	0.090 (3.50)	0.001 (2.02)	0.16 (1.26)	0.32	264
(18) Fixed Effects Estimator, Estimation by Weighted Least Squares		0.44 (8.59)	0.42 (6.32)	0.093 (4.27)	0.002 (3.15)	0.0007 (0.70)	0.44	265

1. **Variables:** Y = real GDP; E = total employment; K = private sector capital stock; R = private sector expenditure on Research and Development; O = share of total trade (imports + exports) in GDP; S = intra industry trade index; I = share of area trade in total trade which takes into account successive enlargements.
Sample: Yearly data (1970-95) for eleven EU countries (Luxembourg excluded). T-statistics in parenthesis.
Source: OECD.

cally when the integration variable is introduced (equation 6). This is understandable, given that (I) is in part a proxy for intra-industry trade inside the Community. On the other hand, the integration variable is positive but never significant. Hence, there is no evidence on pooled data of an additional independent impact of regional trade integration.

Notes

1. The sample covers eleven countries, *i.e.* Belgium, Denmark, Greece, France, Germany, Ireland, Italy, the Netherlands, Portugal and Spain and the United Kingdom. The source of the data are the OECD, Analytical database (ADB) and Foreign Trade Statistics (FTS) database.
2. The intra-industry trade index is defined as the change in the unadjusted Grubel-Lloyd index for all goods. This index calculates the part of balanced trade (overlap between imports and exports) in all trade for a given product j:

   i.e. $S = 1 - \dfrac{\Sigma_j |X_j - M_j|}{\Sigma_j |X_j + M_j|}$, where X and M denote exports and imports.
3. The variable is constructed as each country's share of intra-EU6 trade over its total trade from 1970 to 1972, while intra-EU9/10 trade is considered from 1973 to 1985, intra-EU12 from 1986 to 1994 and intra-EU15 for 1995.
4. There is vast literature on the methodological problems associated with the measurement of intra-industry trade and debate on the use of Grubel and Lloyd type indicators (see for example Fontagné and Freudenberg, 1997). Vona (1991), on the other hand, argues that regardless of its shortcomings, the unadjusted Grubel and Lloyd index is to be preferred in the empirical analysis of intra-industry trade.
5. For a discussion of the use of panel data to estimate production functions see Griliches and Mairesse (1995).

OECD PUBLICATIONS, 2, rue André-Pascal, 75775 PARIS CEDEX 16
PRINTED IN FRANCE
(11 2000 18 1 P) ISBN 92-64-18536-4 – No. 51441 2000